The Unexpected

The Frontiers of Theory

Series Editor: Martin McQuillan

Visit the Frontiers of Theory website at www.euppublishing.com/series/tfot

The Unexpected

Narrative Temporality and the
Philosophy of Surprise

Mark Currie

EDINBURGH
University Press

To Tory, with love

© Mark Currie, 2013

Edinburgh University Press Ltd
22 George Square, Edinburgh EH8 9LF

www.euppublishing.com

Typeset in 10.5/13 pt Sabon
by Servis Filmsetting Ltd, Stockport, Cheshire, and
and printed and bound in the United States of America

A CIP record for this book is available from the British Library

ISBN 978 0 7486 7629 3 (hardback)
ISBN 978 0 7486 7630 9 (webready PDF)
ISBN 978 0 7486 7631 6 (epub)
ISBN 978 0 7486 7632 3 (Amazon ebook)

The right of Mark Currie
to be identified as author of this work
has been asserted in accordance with
the Copyright, Designs and Patents Act 1988.

Contents

Series Editor's Preface

Since its inception Theory has been concerned with its own limits, ends and after-life. It would be an illusion to imagine that the academy is no longer resistant to Theory but a significant consensus has been established and it can be said that Theory has now entered the mainstream of the humanities. Reaction against Theory is now a minority view and new generations of scholars have grown up with Theory. This leaves so-called Theory in an interesting position which its own procedures of auto-critique need to consider: what is the nature of this mainstream Theory and what is the relation of Theory to philosophy and the other disciplines which inform it? What is the history of its construction and what processes of amnesia and the repression of difference have taken place to establish this thing called Theory? Is Theory still the site of a more-than-critical affirmation of a negotiation with thought, which thinks thought's own limits?

'Theory' is a name that traps by an aberrant nominal effect the transformative critique which seeks to reinscribe the conditions of thought in an inaugural founding gesture that is without ground or precedent: as a 'name', a word and a concept, Theory arrests or misprisions such thinking. To imagine the frontiers of Theory is not to dismiss or to abandon Theory (on the contrary one must always insist on the it-is-necessary of Theory even if one has given up belief in theories of all kinds). Rather, this series is concerned with the presentation of work which challenges complacency and continues the transformative work of critical thinking. It seeks to offer the very best of contemporary theoretical practice in the humanities, work which continues to push ever further the frontiers of what is accepted, including the name of Theory. In particular, it is interested in that work which involves the necessary endeavour of crossing disciplinary frontiers without dissolving the specificity of disciplines. Published by Edinburgh University Press, in the city of Enlightenment, this series promotes a certain closeness to that spirit: the continued exercise of critical thought as an attitude of inquiry which counters modes of closed or conservative opinion. In this respect the series aims to make thinking think at the frontiers of theory.

Martin McQuillan

Acknowledgements

The Unexpected continues from my earlier book *About Time*, also published in this series. The idea was the secret sharer in that earlier argument about anticipation and futurity in narrative, and I am very grateful to Edinburgh University Press, and particularly to Martin McQuillan and Jackie Jones for allowing them to sit together on the list as companions. There are many others who have responded to the material as it developed or invited me to present it at seminars or conferences, and I am particularly grateful to Rebecca Beasley, Laura Marcus, Jesse Matz, Jane Elliott, Drew Milne, Randall Stephenson, Amy Elias, Sebastian Groes, Sean Matthews, Kuisma Korhonen, Sarah Dillon, Craig Bourne and Emily Caddick. I am deeply grateful in lots of different ways to friends and colleagues who have shaped the content of this book, or helped me in the writing, or just plain helped me; I particularly want to thank Patricia Waugh, Derek Attridge, Jean Boase-Beier, Stephen Benson, Andrew Cowan, Jeannette Baxter, Robert Eaglestone, Suzanne Hobson, Rachel Bowlby, Giles Foden, Tina Chanter, Ruth Ronen, Ken Newton, Michèle Barrett, Jacqueline Rose, Paul Hamilton, Shahidha Bari and Geoff Ward. I was part of a six-week seminar led by Frank Kermode at the School of Criticism and Theory in 1990 on the subject of literary value; the debates and issues discussed in that group surface repeatedly in this argument, and I would like to thank all those involved, so many years later, for an enduring influence. An earlier version of Chapter 9 appeared in *Kazuo Ishiguro* (Matthews and Groes 2009). Several other people read and responded to this work while in progress, and I would like to thank David Herman, David James and Markman Ellis in particular for being brilliant readers. Special mention must go to the wonderful students of Queen Mary, University of London, who have been a source of constant insight and surprise.

Mark Currie

Introduction: What Lies Ahead

In what lies ahead there is a central claim about the temporality of narrative: namely, that it operates according to a tense structure quite different from the one we normally assume for it. This tense structure is the future perfect, the tense that refers to something that lies ahead and yet which is already complete, not what *will happen*, but what *will have happened*. There is a hint of the impossible in the future perfect. It seems to ascribe to the future the one property that it cannot possess, but it will be my claim that this hint of the impossible, of a future that has already taken place, not only offers us an account of narrative temporality, but also tells us something about how we use stories to reconcile what we expect with what we experience, the foreseeable with the unexpected.

The idea of tense structure, in this sense, follows Genette in *Narrative Discourse* when he says that we should 'organize, or at any rate formulate, the problems of analyzing narrative discourse according to the categories [i.e. tense, mood, voice] borrowed from the grammar of verbs' (Genette 1980, 30). Just as the notion of first person narrative voice borrows its analytical concept from the conjugation of the verb, so tense structure can borrow the specific structures of temporal reference from tenses; and just as the notion of first person narrative voice is not in any way pronoun-dependent, so too is a tense structure capable of indifference to the tense forms of actual narrative verbs. In the case of tense, however, the borrowing might be thought looser. It might be possible to describe a narrative as first person even where there are no first person pronouns, but such a narrative would be unusual: there is a general prevalence of, though not a logical dependence on, the 'I'. In the case of tense, we need to acknowledge a more general mismatch between verb forms and temporal reference at the level of the sentence, and this is also true at higher levels of narrative discourse. To claim that narrative operates according to a tense structure called the future perfect is to borrow temporal properties from a tense that is almost never used in narrative sentences, which differs drastically from the default past tenses of narrative, and offends against our most basic definitions. We normally assume something close to the opposite. We agree with William Labov that narrative is 'one method of recapitulating past experience', and assume that its tense structures are, like its tenses, basically retrospective. To think about narrative as the future perfect is not to think about what we normally think of as tense at all: that is, as a description of the basic relation between the time of an utterance and the time to which it refers. It is to acknowledge instead that narrative is a transaction between some recapitulation of past experience and a reading process in which that capitulation of the past is re-experienced, its retrospect decoded in that process as a quasi-present. Tense is one of the things that narrative theory can borrow from the grammar of verbs not only because it describes aspects of the relation between the time of telling and the time to which it refers, but because it can go further than that. Tense can help us to think about this strange mingling of retrospect with presence, as well as the blend of futurity and the already complete, that come about in the reading of a narrative. It can help, in other words, to describe what is sometimes called, in contemporary narratology, *temporal engagement*: which is to say, a dynamic interaction between the cues of verbal structure and the process of reading. This activity of comprehension, that may or may not take its cues from the grammar of the verb, is focus of this study.

This idea of tense, this expansion of tense, is one of the things that we borrow from the grammar of the verb, but it is not the only thing we need for the description of narrative temporality. A study focused on the idea of the unexpected is a study focused on the future, on the way that we anticipate and fail to anticipate what lies ahead, and the grammar of the verb has other conceptual resources that can be drawn upon that are particular to the issues of futurity. Many would argue that the grammatical category relevant to futurity is not tense at all, but modality, not least because, in English, so the argument goes, there is no future tense. In a language that has no tense morpheme, no ending, for the expression of future events, futurity is carried by modal expressions and temporal indicators, and these are capable of expressing almost infinite gradations of certainty, probability and commitment about the future to which they refer. Just as the future perfect tense is one that we would not normally associate with, or find in, narrative sentences, so too modal expressions (which add words such as *will, must, should, ought, may, might* or *could*) are not what we would expect from the declarative, retrospective default settings of narrative, which deals in what has happened more than what might happen, and with facts more than with possibilities. Modality, especially modal expressions that carry uncertainty, might not be an obvious feature of narrative discourse, but, like the concept of tense, the concept of modality can be scaled up to describe something above the level of the verb or sentence about the dynamics of doubt, uncertainty and knowledge that give narrative its sense of temporal movement. It is clear that some narratives move from mystery to explanation, and so involve some kind of progress from not knowing to knowing as the future of the sequence diminishes and the unread steadily transforms into the already read. This is a useful starting position from which to consider the value of modality to an understanding of narrative time flow, and it is supported by arguments in semantics that modality is the most basic category by which we can understand the passage of time in discourse. According to this view, the impression we have of time flow when we read is produced by the passage from uncertainty to certainty, so that, as the future becomes actualised in the present of reading and passes into the already known or the already read, it models the flow of real time from future to past. It is only a starting position, and runs into problems not only because there are many narratives that do not move from mystery towards explanation, in which progress is a process of increasing bafflement, but also, perhaps more importantly, because it links the question of certainty to questions about what we know and when, or the distribution of knowledge and the structure of disclosure of any given narrative. If we are going to use the concept of modality to describe narrative we will have to link it to this question of the distribution of information, or the perspectival structures of narrative, as well as to other questions about expectation and foreknowledge that are not always wholly controlled by the narrative itself. Like tense, the concept of modality has to expand in such a way that it brings those aspects of the grammar of the verb concerned with probability and certainty to bear on the perspectival structures of narrative, and the effect that they have on the way we think about, perhaps even conceptualise, the future outside of written stories.

Tense and modality have their place in the discussion to come, particularly for the way that they can be used to link narrative temporality to the experience of time in life. At times I will speak of a tense narratology, and this in itself signals the importance of grammar for the analysis, as well as for the philosophical understanding of narrative. But that signal is not a straightforward acceptance of the authority of grammatical or linguistic terminology, and it may at times be necessary to distance myself from the strongest affiliations that exist in contemporary narratology to linguistics. There is a larger point here about the direction that narrative theory has taken since Genette and others formulated this project to analyse narrative according to categories borrowed from the grammar of the verb, and particularly in the light of the energetic refurbishment of linguistic categories that has taken place in the name of cognitive narratology in recent times. If the early pioneers of narratology saw linguistics as their global science, those who pursue narratology as one of the cognitive sciences have often done so by re-establishing linguistics as the preeminent enquiry into the mind and its processes. Those earlier phases in the history of narratology, when, for example, Genette, Jacobson and Barthes called for this kind of borrowing from the description of sentences for the analysis of narrative, are now commonly referred to as the classical moment of narratology, a phase which comes to an end in the various kinds of assault upon the scientific authority of linguistics that are generally associated with poststructuralism in the mid-twentieth century. However we understand this break, what is now often referred to as postclassical narratology has marked its difference from the classical phase by rejecting many of the debilitating assumptions of the classical, structuralist phase. Prominent amongst these abandoned assumptions are the excessive and wrongheaded attitudes that prevailed in structuralist linguistics and, by extension, in classical narratology, to the question of reference in language, which found their way into the study of narrative as the bearers of what now seem perplexing propositions that narrative somehow failed to refer to the world. Postclassical narratology is by no means the only area of literary studies that moved away from such propositions and assumptions, but it has provided some of the most technical arguments with which to overturn the structuralist moratorium on referential issues. It seems important to acknowledge here that the linguistic models that presided over classical narratology were partial and limited in the way that they drew upon linguistic theory, and that their borrowings were often unreliable invocations of the authority of linguistics. Postclassical narratology, by contrast, has encompassed a much broader knowledge of linguistic sources, and most importantly, has turned to arguments in semantics that challenge and reject the reductions of these earlier models. I want to argue that, for all the intellectual reinvigoration that has resulted from these postclassical tendencies, there is also an unnecessary and limiting exclusion, a reluctance to incorporate insights which derive from the philosophical traditions that were most involved in questioning the authority of linguistics in the first place. Some of these excluded perspectives are those that were most influential in the critique of structuralism and its linguistic model, and which came from phenomenology, and Derrida's critique of phenomenology in the mid- to late twentieth century, but, perhaps more importantly, the kinds of perspective that are still flourishing in the twenty-first century that emerged from them. In what lies ahead, I am going to argue that an understanding of temporality needs these perspectives, and that in the analysis of futurity in particular we find a test case for the importance of a more integrated narratology. To my mind, this is one response to the question of how to understand the orientations of contemporary narratology: that a contemporary narratologist must be one who responds to the poststructuralist challenges that were laid against structuralist approaches to narrative, and develops the temporal turn that was at the centre of their critique. To refine the proposition further, the argument ahead is concerned to show that an understanding of narrative temporality, in fictional as well as conceptual and cognitive contexts, can find many of its analytical resources in what can be called the philosophy of surprise.

Before taking these questions more slowly, there is something else that can be said quickly about focusing on the unexpected. I began this introduction with the suggestion that the future perfect offered a temporal structure with particular relevance for narrative, but in what follows it is the relationship between the future perfect and the unexpected that repeatedly comes into focus. If the future perfect, or future anteriority, designates an uncertain blend of futurity and pastness that happens when we read, the unexpected also seems to have some necessary connection to the telling or reading of stories. Studies of storytelling in everyday conversation show that the relaying of an unexpected event is one of the primary functions of narrative, to the point where the mere staging of a narrative in conversation produces the expectation that something unexpected will have taken place by the time it is over. This is one version of the relationship between the future perfect and the unexpected, that what will have happened is something unexpected. The very telling of a story, especially an unsolicited story in everyday life, can produce expectations of the unexpected, or a kind of foreshadowing of the unforeseen. We can note also that a similar paradox hangs over Aristotle's account of tragic plots, or at least what he calls 'complex' plots, which are instructive exactly because they get to their destination through an unexpected route. The future perfect, then, suggests a kind of doubling of temporal perspective, of what will happen with what has already taken place, which is also observable in the notion of narrative surprise, and which seems central to many of the most influential approaches to narrative, whether they occur in everyday or literary settings. There is, in other words, an important proximity between the two notions and the kind of double structure that they impute to narrative time, which nevertheless cannot be thought of as an identity, and, for this reason, they must be thought about together. This is one way of identifying the importance of the philosophy of surprise as a resource for the analysis of narrative, since we find this relationship, this tension, between the future anterior and surprise in many recent philosophical approaches to time. In Derrida's work, for example, there is an early interest in future anteriority that transforms slowly into a preoccupation with messianic time, or more specifically with what he calls the 'messianic without content', by which he designates a certain kind of unforeseen, and yet expected, arrival from the future. This is one of the philosophical contexts that this study aims to bring to the notion of surprise in narrative, but there are versions of the same kind of tension in philosophical thinking about events, about *the event*, in Bergson and Levinas, as well as perspectives that have gained influence more recently through the writings of Badiou and Žižek. These contexts can seem quite distant from the immediate concerns of narrative theory, yet their concerns with the temporality of action and responsibility are often those that we find writ large in narrative, in the paradoxes that surround the future anterior and the unforeseeability of events. If the notion of tense is to be expanded to account for the relationship between narrative and lived experience, these are contexts that help our crossings from storyworlds to life, or from the modelling of time in narrative to the notion of temporal flow in general.

If surprise is a necessary supplement to the future anterior in thinking about narrative, it is also the not-so-secret sharer in our notions of the contemporary. It was always one of the least credible tenets of postmodern literary and cultural theory that we should think about the contemporary as a condition of blocked futurity, in which novelty is reduced to the simulation, repetition and recycling of past forms. Some of this thinking can be attributed to straightforward misreading, of the kind that finds in Derrida's critique of origins, or of genetic thinking about time, a proposition that originality is defunct as a concept, or finds in his account of the archive, the crypt and the ghost a preoccupation with traces of the past in the present. Nobody has written in a more sustained way about the future than Derrida, or engaged with the eschatological tendencies in contemporary thought more critically. The *avenir* is Derrida's preoccupation, and one of its strands is an interest in the future anterior as it bears on expectation and responsibility. One of the most fruitful lines of enquiry into the notion of the contemporary can be found in the use that others have made of this tense to describe an epochal temporality – some distinctively contemporary experience or understanding of time – and to delineate its relations to the thematics of writing. Most famously, in Kristeva and Lyotard, the future anterior is advanced as a tense for our times, and less obviously it is explored by others as a description of temporal becoming, or as a way of being that records the present as future memory, and these future-orientated approaches stand as correctives to those depictions of postmodernity that emphasise its orientation towards the past. But we do not need Derrida's shift towards the concept of messianicity to demonstrate the supplementary value of surprise to these conceptions. However much the notion of future anteriority may have taken hold, in different guises, as an understanding of epochal temporality, it can only be viewed as a specialist interest in comparison to the idea that we inhabit an epoch characterised by the unexpected. It is important to speak here of a notion, or an idea, a certain kind of understanding that a global culture has of itself, rather than of a temporal condition, so problematic is the notion that the contemporary world is somehow more unpredictable than it used to be. But the existence of the idea is difficult to contest, as is the prominence of *unforeseeability* as a criterion of newsworthiness in the context of global news, of a kind that bestows an epochal canonicity upon the unexpected event. It is also important to attend to the kind of credibility that this idea can derive from the notions of uncertainty and unpredictability that have gathered momentum in the physical and theoretical sciences in recent decades, in quantum mechanics and math-ematics, in theoretical physics and evolutionary theory, as well as the applications of game and chaos theory to the unpredictability of economic systems. Some of these areas of enquiry have had to reconcile themselves to the unknowable, and to the natural opacity of the future, while others have inadvertently constructed the category of the unex-pected as a state of exception among the predictive laws that they have established. These issues are relevant to my discussion firstly because of the relation they advance between successful prediction and unexpected events, where the unexpected comes into view exactly because of the increasing sophistication of prediction, and secondly because they suggest that surprise is already well established as a category in the description of contemporary experiences of time. There is certainly a burgeoning section of the contemporary publishing industry, in eco-nomic and social commentary, devoted to this kind of connection between the accommodation of unpredictability in scientific method and the unforeseeable economic events of the early twenty-first century, and some of these works figure in the discussion ahead. But we should rec-ognise also that there is a more serious end to this, which has brought exactly this kind of thinking about unpredictability, spontaneous erup-tion, interruption, reversal of fortunes, eventhood, emergence and change into contemporary political philosophy as part of the effort to think about the relation between unexpected events, futurity and social change. It is as if recent thought, especially where conducted under the banner of the postmodern, has offered an account of only one face of contemporary epochal temporality, of our understanding of our own time-consciousness, concerned with the repetition of what we know. The other face is the unexpected, and in order to think about it, we need to reinstate the future, and, it will be argued, particularly the future that cannot be foreseen, in our conceptualisation of the epochal present. It is one of the convictions of the argument ahead that thinkers who are engaged with narrative surprise bring a special expertise to the wider question of the unforeseeable, and to the dynamics of prospect and retrospect in which the unforeseeable is necessarily experienced and comprehended.

PART I
Surprise and the Theory of Narrative

Chapter 1

A Flow of Unforeseeable Novelty

Special problems attach to thinking about what has not yet taken place, and it is far from obvious that the theory of narrative should have anything to say about those problems. But that is what this book aims to do: to consider the role of narrative in our conceptualisation and our cognitive control of the future, and to explore the experience of reading fiction in relation to the idea of time flow.

The problems, at first sight, mainly derive from the non-existence of the future: from the fact that thinking about what has not yet taken place differs from thinking about what has happened and what is present because the object of reflection is non-actual, or non-existent. There is an essential emptiness about thoughts with a future-orientation – expectations, anticipations, predictions – because they refer to something that may arrive in a different form, and a kind of provisionality, because they must wait upon the arrival of the object to which they refer for affirmation. Because the future does not exist, thinking about the future exists in a state of suspense, waiting for its arrival, and for the object of thinking to pass from virtuality into actuality.

The idea that we wait for the future to arrive, to come into existence or to become actual is full of problematic suppositions. The future differs from the present and the past not only, as Bergson described it, in being non-actual; it is also open, and in being open, it is subject to our efforts, desires and will. One problem with the idea of waiting for the future to arrive is that it assumes a very passive relation to the passing of time. Human subjects are usually busy arranging the future, or actively determining it through their actions in the present. Derrida liked to distinguish between the future that we can predict and the one that actually arrives, but both of these futures are somehow removed from the everyday, active shaping of the future in which most human subjects are constantly engaged. There is a sense in which this relationship between the active shaping of the future and the passive prediction of what will take place, or between acting, striving, planning and arranging on one hand and waiting on the other is exactly the relationship that narrative theory ought to take as an object of enquiry, since it points to a key difference between, and therefore an issue about the relationship of, living and reading. It may be that, in the conduct of our lives, and in our conceptualisation of time flow, we adopt both active and passive relations to future time, working to shape what is to come, and waiting for it to come. It may also be that the distinction between the active and the passive, between acting and thinking, or between working and waiting, is difficult or even impossible to draw. The distinction, nevertheless, has a use for the narrative theorist because it defines a fundamental difference between temporality as it is experienced in life and temporality as it is modelled in written narrative: that in life the future is open, whereas in writing the future already exists.

What does it mean to say that the future already exists in written narrative, or that it does not exist in life? The easy answers to this question are the ones that most expose the assumptions it makes about futurity. It could be said, for example, that there is an obvious difference of access: that wherever we are in the reading of a written narrative, we have access to the future, to what lies ahead of us in the discourse, in the sense that it is there to the right, lying in wait for us to reach it, and it can be visited out of turn, whereas in life, the future is absolutely inaccessible. A second answer follows from this: that whereas in life the future is subject to our efforts, plans and will, in the act of reading, no amount of effort, or planning or willing will influence what is to come, because it is already written and so is unalterable. There are two assumptions that these answers expose. The first is that there is something analogous to time flow in the experience of reading, with an experiential present sandwiched between a fixed past and an unknown future. The second is the assumption that, in the case of the written narrative, what is meant by the future is what lies ahead in the linguistic sequence of words and sentences that constitute the discourse, which may or may not be the same thing as the future of the time sequence referred to by those words or sentences. Both of these assumptions are easily challenged. It could be argued that what lies ahead in a written narrative is not properly thought of as the future at all, because it has already taken place, because it exists, and therefore is not open. Equally, it can be argued that what lies ahead in a discourse might or might not be the future, in the sense that what lies ahead in a narrative is very often a disclosure of something from the past, and that the progress of the linguistic sequence does not necessarily entail the progress of the temporal sequence to which it refers. If these are problems for the idea of narrative as a model of time, they are good problems in the sense that they give direction to the enquiry into the semiotic modelling of time in narrative. The fact that the future is not the future in narrative, because it has already taken place, or is not necessarily the future, because the temporality of a linguistic sequence has to be distinguished from the time sequence to which it refers, offers important foundational premises for an understanding of narrative in relation to time. If we were to consider the discovery that, in written narrative, the future is not the future to be catastrophic to the enquiry, we would be unable to say anything about the relationship between narrative temporality and the lived experience of time. If, on the other hand, we take this fundamental difference as the object of interest, we open up a set of questions about the function of narrative in our understanding of the future, and its effect on internal time consciousness in general. The object of enquiry, in other words, is the difference between the temporality of narrative and the temporality of life, and the fact that there is a difference gives shape to more than it confounds the project.

The theory of narrative, and the theory of the novel, that this book advances find their starting point here: that the basic structure of narrative is one that blends what has not yet happened with what has already taken place, or which fuses together two apparently incompatible ideas of the future – the future which is to come and the future which is already there. The very combination of the two lays claim to a philosophical position, pointing to a kind of compatiblism between allegedly incompatible approaches to time. We find, for example, in the notion of the block universe in physics, or in the untensed view in philosophy, approaches to time which hold that the future already exists, or which aim to rid time of the psychologism, the human egocentricity of the notion of the present, and to place all time zones on an equal ontological footing. In this language, narrative can be understood as a kind of conjunction between tensed and untensed accounts of time, or in a more theological language as a projection of human time on to the axis of divine time, in which the future exists and can be known. But where the untensed or theological view of time makes the existent future inaccessible in the present, narrative gives access to a future which is already written in the present, in so far as it can be visited out of turn, or known in the present, and the existence of the future in narrative is, in this sense, not hypothetical and inaccessible, but actual and objective.

There are a number of starting positions that can be extrapolated from this basic structure, which I will set out immediately as the key problems facing the new narratology. The first is that the relationship between an open future, which is still to come, and a closed one, which has already happened, is the defining feature for the relationship between a reader and what has traditionally been called a protagonist or any other participant in the action of a written narrative. We know that point of view in narrative distributes knowledge in a way that controls the proximity and the distance of this relationship between a reader and a narrative participant, specifically in the degree of access that a narrative grants to a reader of future events. We know also that certain contextual and generic factors govern the degree of foreknowledge that a reader brings to a story, and that this too determines a reader's position and access in relation to the future of narrated events. Gary Saul Morson makes this point about the double temporality of *Oedipus* in an important study of the subject in 1994:

> On the one hand, we contemplate the structure of the whole, and we see signs of it as the action unfolds. On the other, we also identify with Oedipus and his experience, which, like our own, is lived without knowledge of the future. Lacking such identification with the hero, we would probably lose interest in the play.
>
> Our experience of time in *Oedipus* is therefore double: we can imagine what each act feels like, and we also see what it 'really' is. (Morson 1994, 61)

The doubleness of *Oedipus* is a combination of the godlike distance that comes with knowing the future and the proximity of identification, of imagining how it feels not to know. It may be partly produced by contextual and generic factors which cause an audience to know the story in advance, but just to be sure, the play contains its own foreknowledge in the character of Tieresias, the prophet who equalises access to the future for an audience. As a participant in the narrative, Tieresias relays the temporal gaze of an audience in a way that ensures distance, but this does not prevent identification with a participant whose temporal experience is, 'like our own', blind to the future. The internality of Tieresias in fact ensures that the two temporal perspectives are constantly held in view, especially when Oedipus and Tieresias enter into dialogue; as Morson puts it, one character 'speaks from within the story and one from outside it, and we as audience are constantly aware of both perspectives' (1994, 61). What we need to say about this doubleness for the case of written narrative, as opposed to live performance, is that the already written character of a narrative future is not only a matter of objective access to the text that lies ahead, but of the degree of doubleness that pertains as we work our way through it. We often glimpse this notion of temporal perspective in the analysis of point of view, and it becomes more explicit in the efforts of structuralist accounts of tense structure since Genette, but little systematic attention has been applied to the spectrum, of which Oedipus is an extreme, on which foreknowledge is distributed. In theory, it should be possible to place any narrative on a spectrum with this kind of temporal doubleness at one end and the unexpected at the other, given that both extremes remain caught within a quasi-theological conjunction of temporal experience and the already written. The interest for the theory of narrative in this spectrum is the recognition that the experience of time flow in narrative is produced under these conditions, controlled by the distribution of knowledge, foreknowledge and certainty, and yet the notion of temporal perspective remains a rather obscure corner in the theory of narrative. Narratology needs to ask, in the first place, whether narrative time flow can be properly thought of as anything other than the distribution of knowledge in a linguistic sequence. There is also a more drastic argument, which this study will consider later, that the experience of time flow in life is somehow linguistic, semiotic or semantic, bound up with the encoding of certainty in language that grammarians refer to as modality, or with the kind of narrative devices that control and distribute information across a linguistic sequence. The question of narrative as a model of time, in other words, has to be reciprocated by questions about time as a model of narrative, and specifically by an enquiry into the extent to which the experience of time is marked by the doubleness, the dialectic of what is to come and what has already taken place.

The doubleness of identification and foreknowledge, then, is a basic structure in narrative, whether we possess actual foreknowledge or not. Even when we know nothing of what is to come, we nevertheless know that what is to come has already taken place, that it is already there, and that the reading process will reveal it. The conjunction of identification and foreknowledge contains the relationship between human beings and God, between freedom and fate, and these relationships are inherent in the most basic perspectival structures of narrative. If narrative is repetitively, because inherently, concerned with these relationships, or with the question of the existence and the accessibility of the future, we are prompted to ask why narrative criticism, the theory of narrative, and narratology have not ventured further into the philosophical questions they pose. It is not, of course, the case that questions of human freedom and destiny have been absent from the discussion of narrative or fiction, but rather that their discussion has been overwhelmingly thematic and often without regard for the most basic formal and perspectival structures in which these questions are always embedded. If the point of departure for this study is the proposition that it is the difference between lived time and its narrative representation that defines its importance to conceptual and cognitive structures, this is the second proposition: that the relation of narrative to lived temporality is grounded in formal, grammatical and perspectival structures of temporal reference, and in the most basic predicaments of writing and reading. To venture further into the themes of freedom and destiny in narrative is to turn narratological attention on the very idea of written discourse as a model of time, as well as to establish an enquiry into tense structures, perspectival structures and, as Chapter 6 will explore, questions about modality, possibility and uncertainty in the unfolding sequence of a narrative. The linguistic and narratological conditions in which access to the future is granted and denied to readers progressing through a temporal sequence, then, can be thought of as the new gods, and as the locus of the themes of freedom and destiny in narrative.

The foreseeable and the unexpected

The description of narrative in these terms, as a dynamic between the foreseeable and the unexpected, undoubtedly evokes a number of established preoccupations in literary criticism and theory at the same time as it outlines some completely unexplored problems. The positioning of the audience in *Oedipus* astride human and divine temporalities is a useful formula for the way that a narrative can combine a foreseeable future with the experience of unforeseeability in both a technical and a thematic way. It is also useful for an understanding of the opposite tendency: namely, the degree to which narrative sequences are disposed towards the representation of absolute unforeseeability, or which place readers in positions of ignorance in relation to future events, without the benefit of the double perspective of identification and distance, or of any kind of access to the future. It would be difficult to say which of these temporal perspectives is more common in narrative, but we would certainly want to recognise that the narrative of pure identification, in which a reader or an audience enjoys no benefit of access to the future, is commonplace. Events in such narratives are as unexpected for their readers as for their protagonists, at least from the point of view of the distribution of information, and without the doubleness of identification and foreknowledge, these narratives are dominated by suspense at the expense of irony. There may be some reason to believe that suspense is central to the common conceptions of narrative, more characteristic of everyday narrative practices, that narrative has a basic disposition towards this kind of unforeseeability, or that it is a mode particularly adapted to the representation of unexpected events. We might begin here from a study of narratives in everyday conversation, published by Elinor Ochs and Lisa Capps in 2001, in which the recounting of an unexpected turn is discovered as one of the central features of narratives of personal experience. This is not to say that stories are not used in everyday conversation to relate mundane and routine events, but rather that there are certain features that mark the narration of unexpected events, and often seek to reconcile the ordinary course of expectation with the advent of something unforeseen. Ochs and Capps pay particular attention to the way that narratives of the unexpected establish settings for the unforeseen, and that these settings often foreshadow what is to come in a way that is unfaithful to the temporality of the experience related:

> In relatively linear personal narratives, the settings may foreshadow the unexpected event, even though in the actual experience it transpired without warning. Such settings thus paradoxically anticipate at the time of the telling what was unanticipated at the time of the experience told. (2001, 131)

The foreshadowing of settings in linear narratives must be distinguished from the kind of outright foreknowledge we have of Oedipus's fate, but are capable, nevertheless, of providing quite specific indications of the content of the unforeseen. Ochs and Capps offer the example of a setting which explains the automatic locking mechanism on a door as a way of foreshadowing the unforeseen circumstance of visitors becoming trapped in the back yard with two pit bull terriers. This kind of setting establishes privileged knowledge, shared, for example, by members of the family who know the house, and extends it to any listener. The audience, in this narrative, do not know the future, but they have an expectation established by knowledge of the automatic locking mechanism which foreshadows the unexpected in a way that was not the case for those involved, and in this sense the setting doubles the temporal perspective, providing the audience with a specific expectation of future events while still identifying with the ignorance of the participants. Even without full access to future events, the audience in everyday storytelling situations often experience the doubled relation to time that Morson describes in Oedipus, seeing the whole and experiencing how it must have felt not to, whenever a setting offers some glimpse of the whole story in advance. Expectations of the unexpected are established even without these specific foreshadowings, and Ochs and Capps show that the narration of routine events often functions to establish settings for unexpected turns. There are, of course, situations in which narration is used entirely and only to convey predictable happenings – for example, in the narratives of young children, or in the use of stories in families to account for the events of one's day – but routine events can also signal the coming of something unforeseeable, as they do when the narrative is unsolicited:

> [C]onversational narratives that recount fairly predictable events are usually elicited. These tend to be ritualized language practices, as when family members recount their daily activities, or narratives that an interlocutor is coached into telling. More eventful narratives of personal experience, on the other hand, are usually unsolicited. When interlocutors have something they want others to hear, they generally bid for the floor to launch a telling. (2001, 131)

Signals like this therefore transform the relation of routine events into foreshadows, so that, paradoxically, the ordinary can build dramatic tension as a result of some contextual aspect of the storytelling situation, and it is easy to recognise analogous conditions in which the ordinary functions in fiction or film as preparation for an incident that breaks the routine, signalled perhaps by generic markers, or the very existence of the narrative. As in everyday life, narrative in fiction is inherently disposed towards the relation of the unexpected, and makes use of habitual, repetitive and familiar events as a setting for the unexpected to such an extent that the everyday and the ordinary actually carry within them a foreshadowing of an unforeseeable future. In this way, some degree of foreknowledge can inhabit the ordinary by the very fact that a story is being told, but it is also necessary to identify those elements of context, whether in the storytelling situation in conversation or something to do with the generic expectations that surround works of art, that transform the ordinary into omens.

The recounting of the unexpected experience in conversation has, according to Ochs and Capps, an important cognitive and conceptual dimension: however much such stories might function as entertainment, they are also attempts on the part of their tellers to 'reconcile what they *expected* with what they *experienced*' (2001, 134). There are, by this account, key cognitive functions that are played out in narrative in the sense that narrative can test the legitimacy of expectations in the light of what came to pass, as well as reformulate expectations for the future in the light of the retroactive assessment that narrative stages. If Morson's study of narrative in *Narrative and Freedom* aims at a reconciliation of freedom and destiny, Ochs and Capps explore the domestic end of the same problematic; where Morson infers metaphysical attitudes to time from the greats of Russian literature, Ochs and Capps find in the banalities of everyday conversation the same dynamics of expectation and completion. Both of these poles are important to the present study, which aims to show that metaphysical attitudes to time are at work in narrative wherever it is to be found, and equally that there are cognitive dimensions in narratives whether they operate in novels or for the relation of the mundane. The question of literary value, for example, reappears constantly in this study, partly because the category of narrative surprise encompasses some very ordinary and some very experimental tendencies in contemporary fiction: surprise can be a marker of the most disposable and worthless kinds of fiction as well as the effect of originality and difference. This juxtaposition of Morson's *Narrative and Freedom* and Ochs and Capps's *Living Narrative* serves as an indication that sometimes the question of value obscures the most significant questions about the relation of time and narrative, while at the same time pointing to important crossings between fictional narratives and narratives of everyday life for the conceptualisation of future time and for the cognitive control of expectation in general.

The formula offered by Ochs and Capps, which sees narrative as a place where tellers and listeners 'reconcile what they expected with what they experienced', joins the notion of a future which is still to come with one that has already taken place in a way that partakes of narrative's most basic temporal structure: the conjunction of futurity and completion that is inherent in written narrative. We need to be attentive, however, to the theoretical understanding of the relation of speech and writing that this formula involves. We might note, for example, the emphasis that Morson's study of the novel places on the category of writing:

> In a novel the future in fact is there, already written; we need only skip a few pages. It has the full substantiality of a past event. Novels that do not rely on foreshadowing allow us more easily to suspend this knowledge and so to come closer to representing open temporality; novels that use foreshadowing call our attention to the already written nature of narrative time. In doing so, they may either foreground the artifice of fictional narrative or, quite the contrary, may indicate a Leibnizian appreciation of real-world time.
>
> In life (as I understand it), only prior causation is possible ... But in a world of foreshadowing, events are not only pushed but pulled. (1994, 50)

The 'already written' in this account is the opposite of the open temporality of life, and writing, in this sense, is artificial. We can, of course, forget this knowledge as long as the novel in question does not remind us of the existence of the future, but any foreshadowing will break the illusion of open experience and introduce something as preposterous, in its difference from life, as backwards causation. The passage also contains an important counter-suggestion, that foreshadowing may also carry a theological (Leibnizian) sense that real-world time might also be already written, but in effect this possibility is deemed irrelevant because of the question of access, because in life we cannot skip a few pages. Ochs and Capps, by contrast, belong in a tradition that prefers not to draw clear lines between spoken and written discourse, a tradition that begins, in its modern phase, with Mary Louise Pratt's essay *Toward a Speech Act Theory of Literary Discourse* (1977) and can be traced forwards into the 'natural' narratology of Monika Fludernik, and much contemporary cognitive work that aims to pass freely between literature and everyday narrative. For Ochs and Capps, the 'blurring of boundaries between literary works and oral accounts of personal experience resonates with our view that personal narrative has properties characteristic of other genres' (2001, 33). The element of this conviction that I would like to import into my own study is the idea that certain properties are shared between personal and literary narratives, or, to put it another way, that personal narratives might draw upon literary narratives for their resources and vice versa, but there are also elements that I would want to leave behind. If, for example, the opposition between literary works and oral accounts is partly an opposition of writing and speech, the act of 'blurring' that boundary would be exactly to lose the ability to understand the property of writing that speech so often borrows from when it narrates, and the metaphysical attitudes to time, as the already written, the always already completed. There is too the minor confusion created by an alignment of personal narrative with oral delivery, which is also in danger of losing the importance of the written as a crucial semantic field from which the oral draws its metaphors of a future that is already there, completed and determined. In order to understand the metaphysics of the already written and, most importantly, the way that writing functions as a metaphor that we live by, which is to say, as a way of conceptualising time, we need to preserve and attend to, rather than blur, the boundary between speech and writing. On one hand, then, we would want to preserve the emphasis that Morson places on writing, of the objective and accessible future in writing, as a central tenet of the metaphysics of narrative, but on the other, we would want to summon Ochs and Capps against Morson's supposition that foreshadowing, as a critical indicator of the already written nature of narrative time, is confined to actual writing. We need to turn attention, in other words, to the role that writing plays in the conceptualisation of time, and the way that writing comes to signify metaphorically a future that is already there.

Since Lakoff and Johnson (1980), the importance of metaphor in our most basic conceptualisations has been properly recognised, but it can also be said that, since Heraclitus, the problems of metaphorical conceptualisations have been embedded in the philosophy of time. The philosophy of time is a history of metaphors, a quest for improved metaphors, and an enquiry into the roles they play in our basic conceptualisations, to a degree that can make contemporary fashions in cognitive theory for conceptual blending look like a mere flyer. We might think, for example, of Merleau-Ponty's discussion of temporality in *Phenomenology of Perception*, for its deep exploration of metaphor in the conceptualisation of time, or of Bergson's unease about the metaphorical spatialisations that have dominated the representation of time in philosophy.

Even amidst the clamour of metaphors that have vied for some analytical purchase on the concept of time – the rivers and roads, lines and circles, the blocks and fields, trains, clocks, arrows, ski lifts, the recitation of psalms, the listening to melodies, the strings and holes – writing, and especially the written story, has a special place, and in particular a special role in the conceptualisation of future time. If I might be allowed a moment of Žižekean bathos, we can see its resonance in the contemporary imagination in an advertising campaign by Nike to coincide with the 2010 FIFA World Cup, which looked forward to the event with the slogan 'Write the Future', and looked back on it with 'The Future has been Written'. The injunction to write here is part of a general tendency that Lakoff and Johnson understand as the essence of metaphor, of 'understanding and experiencing one kind of thing in terms of another', in this case understanding the actualisation of future time in the present as writing, as an act of authorship, with the subsequent lapsing of that present into the past, drawing on the immutable characteristics of the already written. The positioning of these slogans, before and after the event, adds the dimension of tense to the base metaphor, with the imperative form of 'write' locating the domain of action in the present moment, the domain of freedom. The 'has been written', on the other hand, makes use of the subtle resources of the present perfect to describe an event in retrospect while joining that event to the present moment, so that the act of writing is in the past but the condition of having been written somehow pertains to the present moment. From the point of view of tense, the imperative form 'write the future' is problematic, in the sense that it is usually understood to make use of the base form of the verb – that is, the untensed infinitive of 'to write' – but the imperative is also understood to operate a bit like an interrogative, in the sense that it 'relates the speaker to the hearer and to the here-and-now, typically in face-to-face interaction' (Downing and Locke 2006, 193). This means that, though perhaps untensed in a formal sense, the imperative carries a high degree of immediacy and presence in its temporal reference, and paradoxically it borrows this immediacy from the face-to-face interaction of speech even while it refers to writing. This is not too troubling a paradox. We need to think here of someone telling us, in speech, to write, exactly because writing connotes the archival permanence that speech lacks. The imperative is also problematic from the point of view of voice since, as the base form of the verb, it seems to belong to the category of neither active nor passive verb forms, but as with the question of tense, the imperative connotes high degrees of activity which, like exclamatives and vocatives, derives partly from the typical face-to-face contexts in which they are used. In other words, the question of voice repeats the issue of temporal reference in drawing upon spoken-language contexts for a connotation that contrasts with the actual content of the imperative to write. It contrasts also with the passive verb form of the 'has been written', where tense and voice conspire to consign freedom, action and presence to the past. If the slogan 'Write the Future' is an injunction to act, and if it draws to some extent on typical face-to-face interactions for its effect, there is some ambiguity, when translated into writing, about whom it is addressed to. The television advertisement offers some disambiguation here by preceding the slogan with images of key participants, from all nations, in the story to come, apparently addressing the injunction to them, and identifying them as its authors, but there is also a more general injunction here, an extension of the presumed addressee, or of the range of participants in the World Cup, beyond the World Cup, and perhaps even beyond the realm of sport. The generality of the slogan – the ambiguity about its addressee, the absence of any reference to football, or to sport – casts the event itself as a synecdoche for temporal experience in general, subsuming football in a call to action of pseudo-philosophical scope. The second, retrospective slogan is also ambiguous in this way: the future may refer back to the moment before the event, when possibilities were still open, in order to point out that the prospective moment has simply lapsed, but it might also refer to the future in general, in some Liebnizian appreciation of the already written character of time, or quasi-theological fatalism. These effects are not caused by grammar alone, but largely derive from a kind of self-referentiality between the temporal reference of grammatical forms and the fact that writing and the future are the predicate and the object of both sentences; 'Win the Football' and 'The Football has been Won', while having the same grammatical qualities, would carry none of the same tensions between speech and writing, and none of the temporal confusion of a future which is in the present, and a future which is already in the past.

In this way, the metaphor 'time is writing' is, as Lakoff and Johnson describe it, not a linguistic comparison, not a mere matter of words, but a *metaphorical concept* (Lakoff and Johnson 2003, 6). Metaphor, from this point of view, is not the outward expression of something in our conceptual structure, but is that conceptual structure, and though we are not always conscious that our concepts are thoroughly metaphorical, language constantly reveals the ways in which we understand or experience one kind of thing in terms of another. It is important, for Lakoff and Johnson, that we are not always conscious of our metaphorical concepts, or that the comparisons they involve have become so natural to us that they cannot properly be thought of as comparisons at all, but rather as the actual structure of our experiences and our conceptualisations. These are *structural metaphors*, where 'one concept is metaphorically structured in terms of another' (2003, 14), and they can be distinguished from orientational metaphors which organise 'a whole system of concepts with respect to one another' and mostly concern 'spatial orientation' of the kind HAPPY IS UP ('I am feeling up today') or HEALTH IS UP ('he is in the peak of health'). Orientational metaphors usually have a physical basis in the sense that they derive from physical experiences or spatial orientations that somehow contain perspectives which act as a metaphorical basis of the concept. Time is one of these systems, and the particular example that Lakoff and Johnson offer in their list of orientational metaphors is that of the foreseeable future event. The citation below presents the basic metaphor followed by typical uses and an outline of the metaphor's physical basis:

> FORESEEABLE FUTURE EVENTS ARE UP (and AHEAD)
> All *up*coming events are listed in the paper. What's coming *up* this week? I'm afraid of what's *up ahead* of us. What's *up*?
> Physical basis: Normally our eyes look in the direction in which we typically move (ahead, forward). As an object approaches a person (or the person approaches the object), the object appears larger. Since the ground is perceived as being fixed, the top of the object appears to be moving upwards in the person's field of vision. (2003, 16)

It is not, once again, that this is in any sense 'only a metaphor', or that the idea of future events as 'coming up' is a mere figure of speech, and rather that the concept of the future *is* a spatial orientation. This example appears in a list, and receives no analytical attention, but it is apparent from what is cited here that it is far from simple. It may be that 'up' is a central orientational concept in the notion of foreseeable futurity, but in two of these examples 'up' is combined with 'coming' in a way that makes 'up' seem subordinate to something else more to do with impending arrival than up-wards-ness in itself. In the third example, 'up' is combined with 'ahead', which, as the discussion of its physical basis makes clear, introduces something distinct from upwardness in the form of forward direction, so that 'up' seems to require either the supplement of an arrival or the movement of forward direction to function in a concept. Interestingly, the example that cites 'up' without an adjunct ('what's up?') simply does not work or belong in this argument, having no obvious relation to future time and a more convincing backwards reference to something troubling that *has happened* (while also undermining the earlier proposition that HAPPY IS UP). There are a lot of elements in this metaphorical system that we might worry about. It seems that 'ahead' is much more important than 'up' in the orientational metaphor, and also that, if events come up as they approach the present, their futurity must consist in their being down or below (down the line, as it were). Lakoff and Johnson acknowledge the existence of these sorts of problems, that the word 'up' can derive from a large number of different orientational experiences, resulting in multiple metaphorical meanings of 'up', and therefore that 'up' metaphors may not cohere with each other. They also recognise that a metaphorical concept is, or can be, only a partial account of the concept as a whole: 'In allowing us to focus on one aspect of the concept (e.g. the battling aspects of arguing), a metaphorical concept can keep us from focusing on other aspects of the concept that are inconsistent with that metaphor' (2003, 10). In saying this, however, the identity that they have insisted on between the metaphor and the concept is undermined, since the concept must exceed the metaphor or must differ from it in having other aspects not included in a given metaphor. This problem is really just a version of the larger methodological problem in Lakoff and Johnson, caused by the insistence, on one hand, that metaphors are not just words but the structure of concepts themselves, and continuing to talk about metaphors as comparisons, expressions, or the structuring of one concept according to another. The idea of a comparison, like the idea of a partial representation of a concept, depends upon the existence of an original concept for which the metaphor is a vehicle, on a dualism of the kind we know as the distinction of signified and signifier, meaning that the concept and the metaphor cannot be conflated in the notion of a metaphorical concept. If the metaphor and the concept were truly conflated or understood monistically, there would be no need to talk about the structuring of one concept according to another, and to do so is constantly to repeat, in the very idea of metaphor, the notion of comparison, and the notion of the externality of words to which Lakoff and Johnson think they are opposed. Taken together with the fact that orientational metaphors produce confusing or incoherent systems for understanding concepts, like time, on the basis of physical experience, these slippages between monistic and dualistic accounts of the relation between concepts and their metaphors produce contradictions that come into view whenever Lakoff and Johnson deal with an example.

In the new afterword to *Metaphors We Live By*, written in 2003, Lakoff and Johnson spell out four fallacies about metaphor that go back 'at least as far as Aristotle' and have persisted in the 'twenty-five years since we first discovered conceptual metaphor':

> The first fallacy is that metaphor is a matter of words, not concepts. The second is that metaphor is based on similarity. The third is that all concepts are literal and that none can be metaphorical. The fourth is that rational thought is in no way shaped by the nature of our brains and bodies. (2003, 244)

One immediately thinks of Derrida's early demonstrations that, no matter how hard Husserl tries to get away from an account of language as externality, no matter how hard he tries to conflate conceptual structure with its linguistic formulation, the vocabulary of the inside and the outside, of ex-pression, of metaphor as the outside of language, reasserts itself. I think it would be fair to say that this question has been pushed much further in philosophy than Lakoff and Johnson are prepared to acknowledge, and that we have, in Husserl, a more rigorously monistic account of concept and meaning. More generally, the supervenience that Lakoff and Johnson are proposing between concepts and metaphors is part of the phenomenological reduction, and more significantly still, part of the critique of that reduction as it occurs in Derrida's extensive discussions of metaphor in the text of philosophy, the rigorous and subtle refutations of the first three fallacies listed above in 'White Mythology' that influenced a whole generation, along with de Man's account of the epistemology of metaphor. In relation to the fourth fallacy, it might be argued that Merleau-Ponty's *Phenomenology of Perception*, first published in 1945, is of crucial importance for its detailed account of metaphor in relation to conceptual structure or for its crucial emphasis on the body and its physical orientations in the comprehension of that relation. This is before we have even turned towards the history of psychoanalysis, or pointed to the profundity of metaphor in conceptual structure that emerges from the work of Freud. Perhaps phenomenology and its critique, poststructuralism, deconstruction and psychoanalysis are encompassed by the concluding remarks about 'postmodernist thought' in the afterword:

> At the same time, what we have discovered is fundamentally at odds with certain tenets of postmodernist thought, especially those that claim that

meaning is ungrounded and simply an arbitrary cultural construction. What has been discovered about primary metaphor, for example, simply does not bear this out. There appear to be *both* universal metaphors *and* cultural variation. (2003, 274)

The suggestion that these two received ideas of postmodernist thought – that meaning is ungrounded and that it is a cultural construction – are refuted by the 'discovery' of both universal metaphors and cultural variation is, in my view, an unworthy reduction of a substantial philosophical tradition and a misdirected counter-argument. The influence of Lakoff and Johnson's discussion is nevertheless not diminished by the self-regard of its afterword, and we need to recognise a certain kind of exclusion, a certain reluctance to engage with poststructuralist writings, that presided over the beginnings of cognitive linguistic approaches and which has continued to impose limits on the theoretical scope of linguistics (for example, on metaphor as 'conceptual blending') in more recent times. The relationship between linguistics and philosophical aesthetics, it will be argued in the discussion that follows, needs to rescue itself from this rather irritable stand-off between postmodernism and cognitive linguistics, and nowhere is the need for dialogue more apparent than in the relationship between cognitive narratology and the philosophy of time. To put this in more specific terms, it is important for this study to be able to think about the way that time is thought of, conceptually structured, according to other concepts – the concept of writing, the concept of narrative or the concept of written narrative – without turning one's back on the rigorous enquiry into that particular metaphor that has developed out of Derrida's readings of phenomenology, his writings on grammatology and metaphor, and which cognitive theory is inclined to ignore without argument. The question of cognitive theory will be followed shortly into the territory of cognitive narratology, its relation to the social and political ideas that emerged from poststructuralism, and its dealings with the topic of temporality. For the moment, there are some further steps to follow in the argument about metaphors of time: the logical dependence of time and narrative, of time and writing, and the idea of time flow in general.

The notion that the future is ahead and the assumption that time goes forward are perhaps the most fundamental orientational metaphors we have, but the fact is that they contradict each other. We might think of the first metaphor, with Lakoff and Johnson, as a human subject moving in a landscape, eyes facing the direction of travel, so that the future is ahead. In this case the subject is moving forward while the landscape moved through stands still. How do we reconcile this with the idea that time moves forwards? It would seem that, in relation to a subject moving from left to right, from the past into the future, time must either be static or be moving in the opposite direction: the direction that would, in fact, be backwards if the person involved were to walk that way. These are perhaps best thought of as different orientational metaphors that we have to choose between, and the existence of this choice has been fully acknowledged in the history of philosophy as the distinction between a now that moves and a now that stands still. But the problem that we are getting at here is not the normal problem, often designated by the terms *nunc movens* and *nunc stans*, terms which can be traced back through Aquinas and Augustine at least as far as Plato, to name the opposition between the flow of time that humans experience and the divine perspective of an eternal now. The opposition of a moving and a standing now can also be used, in a quite different sense, to understand two basic physical orientations to which the human experience of time flow can be related: according to *nunc movens*, 'now' moves through a static landscape like a person walking along a road; according to *nunc stans*, 'now' stays still as time flows from the future into the past. Most of our metaphors for the passage of time contain a tension between these two conceptualisations of movement, but none is more glaring than the notion that time is a river; we can stand in the river, facing upstream, while time flows past, or we can be swept along by the river, hopefully in a boat. This is what Merleau-Ponty says about this ambiguity:

> We say that time passes or flows by. We speak of the course of time. The water that I see rolling by was made ready a few days ago in the mountains, with the melting of the glacier; it is now in front of me and makes its way towards the sea, into which it will finally discharge itself. If time is similar to a river, it flows from the past towards the present and the future. The present is the consequence of the past, and the future of the present. But this often repeated metaphor is in reality extremely confused. For, *looking at the things themselves*, the melting of the snows and what results from this are not successive events, or rather the very notion of the event has no place in the objective world. When I say that the day before yesterday the glacier produced the water which is passing at this moment, I am tacitly assuming the existence of a witness tied to a certain spot in the world, and I am comparing his successive views: he was there when the snows melted and followed the water down, or else, from the edge of the river and having waited two days, he sees the pieces of wood that he threw into the water at its source. The 'events' are shapes cut out by a finite observer from the spatio-temporal totality of the objective world. But on the other hand, if I consider the world itself, there is simply one indivisible and changeless being in it. Change presupposes a certain position which I take up and from which I see things in procession before me: there are no events without someone to whom they happen and whose finite perspective is the basis of their individuality. Time presupposes a

view of time. It is, therefore, not like a river, not a flowing substance. The fact that the metaphor based on this comparison has persisted from the time of Heraclitus to our own day is explained by our surreptitiously putting into the river a witness of its course. We do this already when we say that the stream discharges *itself*, for this amounts to conceiving, where there is merely a thing entirely external to itself, an individuality or interior of the stream which manifests itself outside. Now, no sooner have I introduced an observer, whether he follows the river or whether he stands on the bank and observes its flow, than temporal relationships are reversed. (2002, 477–8)

It is clear, then, that the problems that inhere in the metaphor are not problems of expression but difficulties in the conceptualisation of time itself, and that the notion of time as flow requires either a witness or the attribution of some kind of interiority to the stream itself. In this sense there is a kind of egocentricity built into the orientational metaphor, which Lakoff and Johnson reproduce but do not analyse in their discussion of the metaphor 'foreseeable future events are up'. This is, of course, a problem well known in modern discussions of time, and which lies behind the attempt to think about time without reference to any witness, and therefore without the egocentricity of the concept of 'now' and its elaboration as what Heidegger called the 'ordinary conception of time' as a succession of 'nows'. The alternatives that we know most readily from contemporary engagements with time (the tenseless approach to time, McTaggart's B-series and the block universe), in striving to rid the conception of time of its foundational concept – the present – in the name of objectivity, have repeatedly encountered the logical co-dependence of the alternative on the tensed account that they have sought to displace, perhaps most obviously because there is no available orientational metaphor. The notion of time as a spatial totality, of the kind that Augustine located in the mind of God and that Merleau-Ponty goes on to discuss as an objective field, by definition exceeds the grasp of any embodied orientation. The philosophy of time, in this sense, is the unravelling of orientational metaphors, and the reading of metaphors is conceptual through and through, as a form of access into what Paul Ricoeur calls the 'aporetics' of time. In the case of the river metaphor, this unravelling is largely to do with the tension between an orientation in an objective world and the fact that the 'the very notion of an event has no place in the objective world'. Time, in other words, is not a river, but someone watching a river, someone in a river or as a river, and the most basic notions about the direction of time, the meanings of 'forwards', 'up ahead' and 'coming', are confusing not only because several different orientations are at work, but also because the very objectification of time as a moving landscape requires its subjectification in the eyes of a witness, as the fixed point of the *nunc stans* (in its non-theological sense) or the moving point of the *nunc movens*. In this way, temporality is subjectivity and vice versa, or, to put it another way, there is a logical co-dependence between the notion of time and the notion of the subject which also inheres in all our talking and thinking about time. Nor should we expect spatial orientations to act as a grounding for the concept of time in relation to objective orientations such as 'ahead' or 'up'; the concept of 'up', for example, like the concept of 'event' has no meaning in the objective universe. 'Up' acquires its meaning only when I introduce a witness, or a subject position, into the universe, and when I point upwards into the sky, I am, of course, just as meaningfully pointing downwards, or sideways, or outwards into a universe indifferent to the concept of direction. The absolute subjectivity of all physical orientations is, in fact, the basis on which we can properly advance the thesis that concepts and metaphors are the same thing without slipping back into the dualism of Lakoff and Johnson's 'orientational metaphor', since the meaning of all physical orientations is just as groundless as the meaning of the subjective states for which they purportedly act as an analogue.

We might accept, therefore, that the future is ahead and that time goes forwards, even though they belong to different orientational metaphors, because we can happily live with several different concepts of time. It is perhaps worth remembering that Lakoff and Johnson's metaphor was specifically about the foreseeable future – foreseeable future events are up – and therefore to consider that orientational metaphors might have to adapt to particular conceptual needs. *Nunc stans*, for example, has potential to face its witness downstream, so that time still flows past, but it is the past that is in view, while the future comes from behind the point of observation, and therefore to encode the unforeseeable. Both of these basic orientations, the moving now and the standing now, are in themselves incapable of distinguishing between the foreseeable and the unforeseeable event, since the metaphor of a field of vision, of things that are before and behind the eyes, cannot discriminate between the predictable and the unexpected. To do any kind of justice to the complexity with which we make discriminations of this kind, we need to make use of what Lakoff and Johnson refer to as multiple, incoherent and even contradictory physical orientations which, taken in isolation, are capable of representing only a part of what we might think of as a concept of time. We can also say this about the question of cultural variation in the way that physical orientation is used as the basis of temporal concepts: that such variations represent different encodings of the multiple ways in which time is conceptualised as physical orientation. Here, for example, Kasia Jaszczolt offers a complex account of cultural differences in the positioning of a subject in relation to the flow of time:

> In English, like in most other Indo-European languages, the future is predominantly conceptualized as lying *in front of* the observer; we anticipate and predict what 'lies ahead'. The past is *behind* the observer; we are advised not to 'look back' but instead 'move forward' with our plans and ambitions. But for the Maori, for example, the past seems to be conceptualized as lying in front: *ngara mua* means in Maori 'the days in front' and is used to refer to the past. *Mua* means 'front', but also 'before', 'in advance of', 'formerly', or 'first'. On the other hand, *kei muri* means 'behind' and is used for the future. *Muri* means 'behind', 'the rear', 'the hind part', but also 'the sequel', 'the time to come', 'the future' (see Thornton 1987: 70). Similarly, it has been reported that in Aymara, a language of the Andean region of Peru, Chile, and Bolivia, past states of affairs are talked about in such a way that it is evident that the past is conceptualized as being in front of the experiencing agent. The word for 'past' derives from the lexical item *mayra*, meaning 'eye', 'sight' and 'front'. Analogously, the future seems to lie behind: the word for the future is *q'ipa*, meaning 'back' and 'behind'. Both enter into a phrase with the word *pacha*, 'time'. Evidence from gestures made by Aymara speakers supports this thesis of the conceptualization of the past as lying in front and future as lying behind: the further into the past, the further in front the speaker points. These gestures also correlate with the evidential system in Aymara in that events close to the moment of speaking are more likely to have been witnessed and the speaker can report them with higher probability. So, time is linear and may flow in the same direction as that conceptualized by speakers of English, but the relative position of the time arrow and the observer are different. (2009, 28)

Often this kind of variation is invoked to show that different cultures have different concepts of time, and that these differences are revealed in the way that languages deal with temporal reference. We might be tempted to conclude here, for example, that the future is ahead and the past is behind for speakers of English and the other way around for speakers of Maori or Aymara, but Jaszczolt's conclusion is more sophisticated than that: the direction of time is (or 'may' be) the same, but the relative position of the observer to the direction of flow is different. What this means is that the concept of direction in time flow is unaffected by the position of the observer, just as the direction of flow of a river is unaffected whether the observer looks upstream or downstream. The question of whether time does or does not move forwards, in a cosmological sense, is simply translated here into a set of quasi-physical relations between an observer and the line of time, so that cultural variation amounts to nothing very significant; it merely indicates the default position of a particular culture with regard to the multiplicity of physical orientations that can be used to conceptualise time. Across cultures, then, we can observe the same kind of variation that we can also observe within a single language, either between a static and a moving conception of 'now', or within a static conception, according to the position and orientation of an observer. Perhaps more significantly, the difference that Jaszczolt and others have observed between the future that lies ahead, before the eye, and the future that lies behind, out of sight, is the basis for a distinction between foreseeable and unforeseeable events, since the very notion of the foreseeable is a quasi-visual apprehension of an event in advance of its being present, which is to say before we have reached it (the moving now) or before it has arrived (the now that stands still). This is a distinction we would expect to be internal to any conception of the future, whatever default physical orientation might be used to refer to future events, so basic is it to everyday future-orientations such as prediction, expectation, anticipation, hope, fear and action. Though it might be tempting to infer profound cultural differences in the concept of time from differences of this kind, just as it is from the complex differences that exist in future tense structures between languages, the truth is that orientational metaphors of this kind are, like the existence of future tense forms in particular languages, not the whole story of the way that a language refers to or conceptualises the future, and that the dyad of the foreseeable and the unforeseeable therefore can do no justice to the gradations of certainty and uncertainty that all languages can encode grammatically in references to future time. We will come to explore this in detail, as it operates in narrative and in life, in the course of this book, but we need to dwell longer on the basic idea, at this point, that there are levels of epistemological and ontological commitment involved in the most basic ways in which we refer to the future, and that these are generally encoded in terms of visibility.

I have remarked already that Derrida liked to distinguish between the predictable future and the future that actually comes about, referring to the first with the traditional French designation of the future as *l'avenir*, and the second, the surprising arrival, as *l'arrivant*. We need also to recognise the way that unforeseeability has functioned as a key idea in most other major philosophies of the present. In order to understand the importance of Derrida's distinction, which is, at first sight, the most banal of recognitions, it might be necessary to think about philosophers less inclined to recognise any sharp opposition between the foreseeable and the unforeseeable. Bergson, for example, seems much less sure that we can uphold this distinction, since all future events, whether we anticipate them or not, exist, in a sense, in a condition of absolute unforeseeability. Time, for Bergson, is a 'continuous creation of unforeseeable novelty', where that novelty is experienced constantly by all who are alive, and is in no way diminished by the expectation that something will happen:

> No matter how I try to imagine what is going to happen to me, still how inadequate, how abstract and stilted is the thing I have imagined in comparison to what actually happens! The realization brings with it an unforeseeable nothing which changes everything. For example, I am to be present at a gathering; I know what people I shall find there, around what table, in what order, to discuss what problem. But let them come, be seated and chat as I expected, let them say what I was sure they would say: the whole gives me an impression at once novel and unique, as if it were but now designed at one original stroke by the hand of an artist. Gone is the image I had conceived of it, a mere prearrangeable juxtaposition of things already known! I agree that the picture has not the artistic value of a Rembrandt or a Velázquez: yet it is just as unexpected and, in this sense, quite original. (2002, 223)

Even the most expected things are unexpected, in the sense that they replace the abstract and stilted image of what is to come with something novel and unique. This gap between what we expect and what actually happens, this unforeseeable nothing which changes everything, abolishes the distinction between the foreseeable and the unexpected. The ordinary is as original as art because it differs, every time, from expectation, and in this sense the expectation itself is the vehicle of unforeseeable novelty. But the unexpected here is nothing more than the difference between the kind of image that we have to form in order for expectation to take place, and the novelty of what actually arrives, or between the phenomenal vagueness of an expectation and the appearance of an event in the present, and in this sense events are universally unexpected. This account of time, as the continuous creation of unforeseeable novelty, is one that philosophers have been, according to Bergson, unable to accept:

> The ancients already revolted against it because, Platonists to a greater or less degree, they imagined that Being was given once and for all, complete and perfect, in the immutable system of Ideas: the world that unfolds before our eyes could therefore add nothing to it . . . The moderns, it is true, take a quite different point of view. They no longer treat time as an intruder, a disturber of eternity; but they would very much like to reduce it to a simple appearance. (2002, 232)

The words 'complete' and 'perfect' are interesting here because temporal meanings hide within them: not only do they mean 'whole' and 'ideal' respectively, but they both also refer to events that have already taken place. This is the *perfectus* of grammatical tense – of the future perfect, for example – which designates completed action, of what will have happened, and the truth of time, for the ancients, involved no unfolding, flow or movement of the kind to which human being is confined. The moderns, on the other hand, have a similar constriction, not by locating the truth of time in the immutable system of Ideas, but rather by reducing it to a simple appearance: something before the eye in a way that is comparable to the *nunc stans* of Platonic Ideas or divine eternity – something, in other words, that will stand still for a moment, and so arrest the continuous creation of unforeseeable novelty that Bergson takes to be the universal human experience of time. We see here, then, a kind of meeting of the ancient and the modern terminology, the *nunc movens* / *nunc stans* distinction of ancient and medieval philosophy, and the reduction of movement to an appearance, which we find everywhere in the philosophy of time from Augustine to modern phenomenological approaches: both, for Bergson, are futile attempts to arrest the continuous flow of the unforeseeable.

Chapter 2

Narratological Approaches to the Unforeseeable

There is narrative theory that concerns itself with the unforeseeable, but not in what might be thought of as the mainstream of contemporary narratology. Questions of surprise, of the unexpected, the reversal of fortune, of chance and contingency are present in the philosophical traditions of writing about narrative and nearly absent from the new, 'postclassical' narratologies and cognitive narratologies that have dominated the systematic and theoretical study of narrative since the mid-1990s. There is a larger issue here, about the absence of a more general kind of any systematic analysis of narrative temporality in postclassical narratology, and within this, a more specific avoidance of questions about the future, not only in terms of the expectations generated in the experience of reading, but of narrative as a mode of expectation, anticipation, or as the basis on which we conceptualise, plan, act upon, control and understand, predict, expect, fear or hope in relation to what is to come. The theory of narrative is inclined to view narrative as recollection, as the indicative representation of things that have happened, without regard to the questions of what will happen, or what will have happened, in the future. The general absence of these questions, particularly of questions about surprise, in narratology is surprising itself, for two reasons. In the first place, in the light of what we have been saying here about the already-there-ness of the future in narrative, we might want to lay claim to the apparent fatalism of narrative as the key feature of narrative temporality as distinct from the temporality of life, and therefore to see the future as the temporal orientation that most gives narrative its distinct temporal properties. In the first place, then, we might be surprised that narratology is not a species of futurology, not in the sense that it should be interested in the ways that future time has been represented or imagined, but in the much more basic sense that narrative exists in a hermeneutic circle with life by virtue of the fact that it differs from life in this key respect: that narrative is the place where the future exists, and yet the most systematic approaches to narrative have remained indifferent to the ontology of future events as an issue. We should be more surprised still about this absence because of the prominence of these questions in contemporary philosophy, where the idea of the unforeseeable, as well as the question about the opacity of the future in general, has been at the centre of thinking about time and the event for several decades.

What is an event, in philosophical contexts, if not the occurrence of the unforeseeable? It will be important to think carefully about the relation of specialised conceptions of the event in philosophy and social theory to the kinds of meanings accrued by that word in narrative theory, but it is easy to support the idea that unforeseeability is the key attribute of those philosophical conceptions:

> The attempt to submit chance to thought implies in the first place an interest in the *experience* (I emphasize this word) of that which happens unexpectedly. Indeed there are those of us who are inclined to think that unexpectability conditions the very structure of the event. Would an event that can be anticipated and therefore apprehended or comprehended, or one without an element of absolute encounter, actually be an event in the full sense of the word? (Derrida 2007, 5)

For Derrida there is a 'full sense' of the word *event*, which I take to mean a specialised sense, which not only encompasses but also is defined by unexpectability. There are three things to note about this statement. First, it is *unexpectability*, not the property of being unexpected, that makes the event what it is, so that the absolute encounter comes about not when something *was not expected*, but when it *could not have been expected*. That the unexpected is not a matter of stupidity, or of some kind of failure of accurate prediction, but a question of something that could not have been predicted will be of importance to the discussion of unexpected narrative events. Second, the unexpected here is linked to the notion of chance, but linked in a very vague relation: that thinking about chance implies an interest in the experience of the unexpected. Because chance is a subject that has preoccupied critics of narrative fiction (but not, to any great extent, narratologists), it will also be important to decide whether there can be chance in narrative, to what extent it overlaps with the category of the unexpected, and what part it plays in the production of narrative surprise. Third, we have to note the unspecified, specialised community responsible for this conception of the event – the 'those of us' who are inclined to think in this way, and reach a decision on whether this conception of the event is relevant to the relation of narrative to life. There is, for Derrida, on the one hand, a specialised group of event philosophers, and on the other, a generalised orientation towards a visible horizon, a universal 'we' for all who experience time according to the metaphor of foreseeability:

> There are those of us who lean toward the assumption that an event worthy of the name cannot be foretold. We are not supposed to see it coming. If what comes and then stands out horizontally on a horizon can be anticipated then there is no pure event. No horizon, then, for the event or encounter, but only verticality and the unforeseeable. The alterity of the other – that which does not reduce itself to the economy of our horizon – always comes to us from above indeed, from the above. (Derrida 2007, 6)

If the idea of a horizon seems to belong to the basic orientational metaphor we discussed in the previous chapter, in which the future lies in front of the eyes in the direction of travel, it also has a more complex philosophical background in Husserl and Heidegger, and then in Levinas. These are issues that we will return to later, in the explorations that follow of phenomenological approaches to the flow of time in life and narrative. What is important to observe now is that the event, in this specialised sense, approaches on a different axis. It comes from above. It approaches on a vertical axis without standing out 'horizontally on a horizon', and on this geometric configuration, the pure event is defined, not only as the unforeseen, but also as unforeseeable.

This philosophical conception of the event, as the unforeseeable, is by no means alien to existing thought about narrative. It can be found in Bakhtin's conception of *eventness*, which is a property possessed only by certain happenings, certain eventful events, or momentous choices that are more than usually involved in the determination of what happens. Morson, in summarising Bakhtin, places emphasis on the momentousness and presentness of choice in the realisation of possibilities: 'When the present simply actualizes what had to happen, events lack eventness' (1994, 22). But Morson is also in no doubt about the role of unexpectability in Bakhtin's eventful event:

> The same act performed later would not be quite the same act. It is therefore constituted in part by important particularities that no abstract and timeless system could foretell. Above all, the eventful event must produce something genuinely new, something beyond a predictable consequence of earlier events. If eventness is real, no knowledge of the past, no matter how comprehensive, would be sufficient for making a perfectly reliable prediction of the future. Bakhtin viewed all of our choices, however prosaic, as having a measure of eventness, and he rejected all models of the world that did not allow for 'surprisingness'. (1994, 22)

On one hand, all choices have a measure of eventness, but on the other, the event must be particular to the point of being unforetellable, and no amount of knowledge of the past would make it expectable or foreseeable. If, for Derrida, the unforeseeable seems connected to chance, for Bakhtin and Morson it is decisively linked to freedom, or to the possibility of momentous choice in the present of a kind that is consistent with surprisingness. Chance and freedom are immediately recognisable as issues that have figured in the discussion of narrative since Aristotle, and it is worth reflecting on the extent to which Aristotle's engagement with tragedy sets the terms for the discussion of surprise in contemporary narrative theory, or still defines the philosophical context for thinking about eventness, the unforeseen and the unforeseeable in the present. In the work of Paul Ricoeur, for example, the Aristotelian notion of emplotment is understood as an act of configuration, or composition, which balances a demand for concordance, or the unity of the plot across time, with discordances, or events that are admitted into the plot and which make up the disparate components of the action. A plot is, therefore, a discordant concordance, and a synthesis of the heterogeneous. These are the terms and phrases that run through the three volumes of *Time and Narrative*, as they work to 'extend the validity of this concept of narrative configuration beyond Aristotle's privileged example – Greek tragedy and, to a lesser degree, epic poetry', as he puts it when he revisits the question in *Oneself as Another* (1992, 141). The summary of *Time and Narrative* that Ricoeur offers in *Oneself as Another* is particularly revealing for the place it gives to surprise in relation to the ordinary idea of narrative events.

'By discordances', Ricoeur says, 'I mean the reversals of fortune that make the plot an ordered transformation from an initial situation into a terminal one' (1992, 141). These reversals of fortune, which Aristotle called *peripeteia*, and might include chance occurrences or conscious choices, are the umbrella under which literary critics have discussed events which turn things upside down in a narrative. Frank Kermode, for example, sees peripeteia as 'a disconfirmation followed by a consonance', the interest of which lies in 'having our expectations falsified . . . by an unexpected and instructive route' (2000, 18). The tradition of thinking about peripeteia is of interest partly because it installs in the ordinary conception of the event an element of the unforeseeable, in the sense that it names the kind of event that enacts a reversal of fortune or expectation, and that this installation derives from Aristotle's account of mimesis as the imitation of action, and therefore from the most ancient accounts we have of the narrative event. For Ricoeur, then, this ancient account of emplotment contains within it the idea of a narrative event as a paradox brought about by the opposing forces of concordance and discordance:

> The paradox of emplotment is that it inverts the effect of contingency, in the sense of that which could have happened differently or which might not have happened at all, by incorporating it in some way into the effect of necessity or probability exerted by the configuring act. The inversion of the effect of contingency into an effect of necessity is produced at the very core of the event: as a mere occurrence, the latter is confined to thwarting the expectations created by the prior course of events; it is quite simply the unexpected, the surprising. (1992, 142)

The importance of the unexpected in narrative is that it reconfigures contingency as necessity, and thus, as he puts it a few pages later, 'chance is transmuted into fate' (1992, 147). The reason that the effect of contingency is inverted, or incorporated in some way into the effect of necessity, and which is not quite spelled out here by Ricoeur, is that narrative combines a representation of what is to come with the representation of what has already taken place, the open future with the scripted future of narration, and so the paradox of concordance and discordance can be reduced to the core paradox of narrative representation: the condition of waiting for events to happen that have already taken place. But we still need to ask: what, then, is the effect of narrative on the lived experience of time, or the relationship between the unexpected event in fiction and the unexpected event in life, given this transmutation of chance into fate, contingency into necessity, and for this philosophical question Ricoeur is more helpful than any other guide.

It is one of the mysteries of contemporary criticism that Ricoeur's work on narrative has so little informed literary critical and narratological approaches to time, and this may indicate a general problem, for narratology, in engaging with the philosophical questions that arise in the crux of time and narrative. Perhaps the most important work on the subject of surprise in recent years is to be found in the writings of Meir Sternberg, whose approach helps us to move the discussion towards narratological contexts, and also to summarise the extent to which questions of the foreseeable and the unexpected have figured in recent theories of narrative. Like Ricoeur, Sternberg is convinced that the problem is outlined for us by Aristotle, but this is not to say that our contemporary theoretical approaches are Aristotelian; rather 'Aristotle's *Poetics* offers in some ways a lure, in others a mirror, in yet others a contrast to present day theorizing about narrative' (Sternberg 1992, 474). For Sternberg, Aristotle is the source of basic questions about the relation between chronology and teleology, or the forward motion of an unfolding plot and the backward movement of our understanding of events, 'first within the arrangement of the "whole" (holos) and, second, within the disarrangements open to "plot" (mythos)'. There are, in other words, two different kinds of question about the relation between forwards and backwards in narrative, the first of which is concerned with the work as a whole, and the second with the order in which events are arranged and therefore experienced by a readership or an audience.

Like Ricoeur, Sternberg identifies surprise as one of the key concepts in Aristotle's approach to the arrangement of events within the 'whole' of a plot, and wants to extend it outwards from the discussion of tragedy to narrative plotting in general. For Sternberg, Aristotle is 'the first and virtually the only one among poetic system builders' to privilege surprise, but not nearly enough:

> [S]urprise is not only among the few narrative interests – together with curiosity and suspense – but also among the still fewer effects that absolutely live by temporal manoeuvring. Aside from any intrinsic importance, I therefore believe, tracing its operations promises to throw invaluable light on the temporality / teleology / narrativity crux . . . Methodologically, it provides a standard whereby to distinguish true from false claims for dechronologizing and, even more elusive, true claims for dechronologizing from false claims against narration by chronology. Theoretically surprise leads straight to the heart of narrative dynamics, uniquely interrelating the communicative with the mimetic process. (1992, 507)

This is an important passage. If Aristotle is, for Sternberg, one of the very few to privilege surprise, Sternberg is, for me, virtually the only narrative theorist to place surprise at the heart of narrative dynamics in this way. But there is a polemic here against the 'claims for dechronologizing' that requires some inspection. There is distaste here for dechronologising, and for the false claims made in its name, as well as a view that surprise belongs to mimetic chronology, that is more difficult to ingest.

Prolepsis, as Genette understood it, might be thought of as the opposite of surprise. It is one of those anachronies, the one that reveals the future out of turn, and because in life the future cannot be revealed out of turn, can be thought of as anti-mimetic. Prolepsis introduces a disjunction in the relation between the communicative and the mimetic process, and this excludes it, in Sternberg's mind, from the heart of narrative dynamics. One of the reasons that surprise needs to be reinstated at the heart of narrative theory is that, for Sternberg, anachronies like prolepsis and analepsis have acquired a strange monopoly over the domains of anticipation and retrospection:

What in reason justifies the monopoly on anticipation given to 'prolepsis' by overt statement, such as a narrator's foretelling or a hero's foreboding of death, at the expense of established (if tacit) convention to the same effect, such as our foreknowledge of the unhappy end in tragedy; or at the expense of straight chronological development, inevitably generating and often polarizing expectations about the future towards which it marches ... ? (1992, 495)

This is a good question. What is the difference, Sternberg asks, between the official, ill-timed visit to the future and the many kinds of anticipation that are in play in straight chronological development? The problem with the question, however, is that it seems to conflate the expectation of an event with the actual excursion into future events of which narrative is uniquely capable. Against Sternberg, I would argue that prolepsis is distinguished from expectation and anticipation in general on the grounds of being an actual, not a virtual, future. Genette's definition of prolepsis is careful to honour this distinction, and so the difference between a proleptic anachrony and a clue or hint. The distinction between prolepsis and anticipation in general derives partly from the former's flaunting of the already-there-ness of the future, and therefore from a profound disjunction between the communicative and the mimetic process. There is also the question of whose anticipation we have in mind, since Sternberg's objection to prolepsis seems also to conflate the narrator's foretelling, the hero's foreboding and a reader's expectation, both of the sequence itself and of the genre in which it operates. In fact, this latter objection is more than a little unfair in respect to the sophistication with which Sternberg addresses the question 'whose surprise?', and I will return to that issue in a moment. For now it is worth noting that there *is* something in reason that justifies the distinction between prolepsis and anticipation in general. Whether it also justifies a monopoly on anticipation given to prolepsis is more doubtful, and there are certainly numerous difficult cases where we cannot be sure whether we have been involved in an untimely, official visit to the future of a chronological sequence. The conflations of actual and virtual futures here, bound up as they are with the question of whose surprise we are dealing with, slightly spoil Sternberg's question, and seem to invite a slightly different one. What difference, after all, does it make if we visit the future out of turn? A common answer to this question, and one that Sternberg offers himself, is that it changes the nature of a reader's future orientation from what will happen to how it comes about – that is to say, from suspense to curiosity, involving us not in progression from cause to effect but in a regression from effect to cause. For Sternberg these are the three generic master roles – suspense, surprise and curiosity – determined by the relation between chronology and teleology both within the arrangement of the whole and within the disarrangements, such as the anachronies, of a plot. But we see here a question to which we will often return in this study about the difference between a work which makes us wait and one that informs us in advance: what is the difference between knowing in advance and waiting for that knowledge to arrive? 'Peripeteia', Kermode tells us, 'has been called the equivalent, in narrative, of irony in rhetoric' (Kermode 2000, 18) and this equivalence might propose that there is no difference, or that if there is a difference it is one of duration alone: that surprise simply strings out over time the doubleness that foreknowledge installs from the start.

Sternberg's preference for surprise over anachrony, as I have said, is a kind of value judgement based in the contract between the communicative and the mimetic process, which is to say that surprise imitates the absolute unvisitability of the future in lived experience. It may be a judgement based in some strategic opposition to the overexcitement around Genette's categories of anachrony, but it is also underwritten by the claim that surprise goes to the heart of narrative dynamics. It is, in other words, a preference for a particular arrangement of *holos* and *mythos*, in which irony is dispersed linearly across a sequence, and requires some retroactive moment at which the significance of earlier events is understood and revised. The whole question of value is worth highlighting here, because we run into it often in discussions of peripeteia, and this is no doubt because Aristotle's own discussion hinges on an apparently evaluative distinction between the 'simple' and the 'complex' plot. The hierarchy of the simple and the complex, however, is not a straightforward question of the imitation of 'natural temporality':

> Chrono-logic itself bends, temporarily at least, in response to a stronger, more determinate teleo-logic. Given that tragedy and high epic aim for pity and fear, then 'such an effect is best produced when the events come to us by surprise' (ibid.: Chap 9). And given the demand for surprise, the 'whole' action needs to be 'complicated' (in effect, as will appear, dechronologized) into 'plot' by way of discovery and / or reversal (ibid.: chaps 10–11). For example, instead of moving directly from happiness to unhappiness, the 'simple' and minimal tragic way, the sequence will promise a happy outcome, only to turn round with a vengeance: the mandatory change of fortune then complicates its route, and compounds its impact, by a sudden change of direction, unpredictable (for surprise) yet in retrospect probable (for wholeness, if only after the event). (1992, 476)

In Aristotle, the value of surprise does not lie in its fidelity to the unknowable future, which might also be a fidelity observed by routine or expected events, but in the effectiveness of events that come on us by surprise for the purposes of instruction or catharsis. We find ourselves in familiar territory here, of Aristotle against Plato on the subject of mimesis, in a debate where literary value is pulled between the values of imitation and instruction, where surprise is the instructive route to a discovery or recognition. Sternberg acknowledges that the distinction between simple and complex plots is not directly translatable into the difference between chronology and anachrony, since surprise itself is effectively a de-chronologising of the simple sequence, but he does want to recruit Aristotle's 'insistence on reserving surprise twists for the complex plot' to the case against 'most contemporary approaches to narrative poetics' and their 'valuation of dechronologizing per se' (1992, 477). However pointless it may seem to try to root literary value in particular arrangements of plot, it must be acknowledged that the effect of Aristotle on the discussion often seems to be to introduce value to the description of structure. Hence, when Kermode observes the equivalence of peripeteia and irony, he also sees it as a figure that is present 'in every story of the least structural sophistication' (2000, 18). Sternberg points this out himself in the work of the Neo-Aristotelians of the Chicago School in the 1950s and 1960s, particularly R. S. Crane and his best-known pupil Wayne Booth, who he admonishes, along with others, for upholding the 'superiority of the complex plot'. Yet it is the alignment of complexity and surprise in Aristotle's account of tragedy that underwrites Sternberg's own claims for the importance of the unexpected in narrative plotting more generally:

> Aristotle does put a premium on surprise as a (or rather, the) contributing factor to tragedy's catharsis; but although this valuation turns out to be too high in terms of his own project, it remains a good plea for complexity and, if anything, needs to be raised still higher within a more general framework. Actually, as the horizon widens from tragic to narrative plotting and temporality, we would do well to invert Aristotle's scale of affective priorities between catharsis and surprise. (1992, 506)

Others may have upheld the superiority of the complex plot, but Sternberg wants to elevate one of its devices, surprise, above the category of catharsis itself when we turn our attention outwards to narrative plotting more generally. For in the affective operations of stories more generally, surprise is the one that takes us, theoretically, straight to the heart of narrative dynamics.

The role of surprise in narrative dynamics takes Sternberg into the heart of a question which the theory of narrative has been oddly reluctant to ask: the question of whose surprise we are talking about.

Aristotle's account of surprise, Sternberg tells us, 'centralizes the producer's viewpoint and works at the expense of the receiver's', and so 'addresses itself to the plot's construction by the artist out of some whole, not to its reconstruction, much less its interpretation, by the reader into some whole' (1992, 513). This is part of a general bracketing of the audience in *Poetics* that make it impossible to think about the two activities, of writing and reading, construction and reconstruction, together. What is lost in this bracketing is partly the very thing that links surprise to prolepsis: that is, a certain switching of forward orientation, toward what will happen, to a backward one, toward how it came about, which takes place in the activity of interpretation in response to surprise, when the 'unexpected future springs an unexplained past' (536). Sternberg also finds in Aristotle the assumption that, for a plot to be probable, surprises must pretend to be surprises that were enacted in real life, as the mimesis of 'an abrupt change of fortune that befalls the dramatis personae themselves', as if there were a real sequence of events to which the art is attending. Again this is a very restricted approach to the question of surprise, since a reader can clearly be surprised to discover something that a protagonist has known all along, and reciprocally, there may be surprises in store for a protagonist that readers have been informed of, or, for numerous reasons, know about, already. There are two questions here, one about the mimetic motivation for surprise, the other about whose surprise we are talking about, that mar many of the existing approaches to the unexpected in narrative temporality. So, for Sternberg, Aristotle's mimeticism persists as a dogma from Renaissance neoclassicism to Vladimir Propp; Genette's analepsis and prolepsis assume an objective chronology from which anachrony departs, as if the objective facts were not themselves mere constructs of the discourse at hand; Bakhtin 'fails to mark off the reader's surprise from the hero's, dramatized from purely discursive recognition' (512); and even Barthes yokes together 'actional and narrational units under the term *function*' (513). The mimetic distinction, then, between the representation and what is represented, the dualism of the narrative and its objective time sequence, tends to obscure the true nature of discursive teleology 'as a two-sided affair transacted between author and audience, telling and reading' (513). It is really when the mimetic dogma surrounding the category of surprise is broken, when we no longer think of it as the representation of something surprising that actually occurred, that the varieties of surprise come into view. No wonder, also, that surprise should become the 'heart of narrative dynamics', since 'the distinctiveness of surprise relates to the manner and point of disordering, not (like catharsis) to the matter disordered into surprise-sequence' (1992,

523). As soon as surprise is understood in this way, not as the representation of surprising events, but as the manner and point of disordering,
everything in narrative falls under its rule. It becomes a question not of
unforeseeable happenings, but of unforeseen disclosures.

In the first place, then, it seems that Sternberg values surprise for its
unique interrelation of the 'communicative with the mimetic process'
and in the second place that he holds mimesis as a kind of limitation on
the value and scope of surprise. We can go some way, via the heresies of
paraphrase, towards a resolution of this contradiction if, for example,
we assume that the interrelation of communicative and mimetic process
is so complete that they are no longer to be distinguished at all, and take
his claim to be that mimesis is nothing more than the arrangement of
discourse itself. But if we do assume that the mimetic and the communicative process are the same thing in Sternberg's argument, we completely
abandon the essential definition of mimesis, and in the process we give
up on the hope of saying anything meaningful about the relation of narrative and life. It will be recalled from the last chapter that the object of
study for my enquiry is the difference between the temporality of narrative and the temporality of life, the interaction between them, and the
hermeneutic circulation of narrative and lived surprises. For guidance
here we need to turn back to Ricoeur's writing on mimesis, and particularly to those places where he explicitly distributes the function of
mimesis between makers and audiences, writers and readers, or events
and discourses. Mimesis, for Ricoeur, as he outlines it in volume one of
Time and Narrative, is not a simple relation between art and life, but a
process which can be broken down into three components or stages.
Mimesis 1 is prefiguration, and refers to some basic, pre-existing human
competence in understanding what action is, an understanding that
allows readers and writers to make inferences about what would
happen, how human agents would act, as well as the cultural traditions
from which plot emerges. Importantly, one of the categories of this pre-
understanding, for Ricoeur, is temporality, which is to say that our
preliminary competence is partly a condition of being-within-time, of
having a certain understanding of what *now* means, and of the basic
future-orientation of lived experience. This pre-understanding is learnt
from the world, and forms the basis on which narrative emplotment is
constructed. Mimesis 2 in this scheme is emplotment, more or less as
Aristotle describes it, as the configuration of narrative elements into an
intelligible whole. Like prefiguration, configuration has definite temporal features, such as the assembling of events into a followable sequence,
the crafting of an ending from which events can be seen as a whole, and
therefore the construction of an alternative view of time, based not on

time flow, or the arrow of time, but one in which the ending can be read in the beginning, and the beginning in the ending, and which teach us to read time itself backwards. Finally, Mimesis 3 is refiguration, and it responds to, but goes beyond a suggestion to be found in Aristotle that it is 'in the hearer or reader that the traversal of mimesis reaches its fulfilment' (1984, 71). Refiguration refers to the way that narrative applies to and modifies the world in the mind of the hearer and reader, and while Aristotle nods in this direction in the *Poetics*, he leaves its fuller study for his more extended discussion of the audience in his *Rhetoric*. As a modification of understanding in the mind of a reader, refiguration completes a circle in the sense that narrative emplotment modifies the world that prefiguration understands in the first place, so that the world of action is modified or marked by narrative in advance. In this sense, mimesis works both ways: emplotment may imitate the world of human action, but human action already bears the marks of refiguration, so that narrative imitates a world of action that itself imitates the world of narrative, and in this reciprocity between mimesis and reverse mimesis, where life imitates art and art imitates life, the hermeneutic circle of narrative and life or, as Ricoeur has it, the circle of narrative and time, revolves. So, for example, the sense of an ending that comes about in narrative emplotment at the point of completion might produce a view of time as a whole (as opposed to an inescapable flow) which teaches us to think about time backwards; this might in turn refigure our sense of lived experience by inflecting it with an anticipatory sense of an ending, of something to come, which would inflect our experience with the properties of narrative time and thus modify that experience in advance. For this reason, when contemplating the circle of mimesis, Ricoeur devotes his attention to the '(as yet) untold stories' that might inflect our experience of time as it unfolds, as if experience itself might be already refigured by a kind of emplotment that it supposedly records. It is not only for this temporal folding, this rejection of mimesis as the representation of a prior and objective sequence, that we should value Ricoeur's circular account of mimesis. The hermeneutic circle between narrative and life also provides a framework which, by distributing the category of surprise between the producer and the reader, helps us to address the question 'whose surprise?', and allows us to extend the enquiry into surprise far beyond the representation of events not expected by particular characters in the fictional universe. Ricoeur's circle includes all the participants in the transaction between authors and an audience, the telling and the reading, into the process of mimesis, and this helps us out of Sternberg's objection that contemporary narrative theory operates under a restricting assumption of some objective chronology of events. Most importantly, it gives us some way of thinking about the relationship between surprise in narrative and the way we think about surprise events in life, since the role of surprise in the configuration of a plot becomes a factor in the refiguration of the world, which in turn structures our pre-understanding of the unexpected event, which might mean, among other things, to understand it backwards, to invert the effect of contingency into the effect of necessity, or to transform the flow of time into the completed whole of a plot.

If Sternberg's view of Aristotle is that he addresses himself, in the *Poetics*, too much to the question of the production of a plot and too little to the question of its reception, Ricoeur's circle of mimesis is a corrective. This is not a correction that merely turns attention to the banalities of an individual reading process, but one that reframes the contract of production and reception as a kind of cognitive interdependence between stories and the world, or, in Ricoeur's language, an existential analysis of human beings as 'entangled in stories', not only because they are ubiquitous, but also because they structure the pre-understanding of temporal experience from which stories supposedly follow. Present experience is, according to Ricoeur, an untold story, the narration of which is a secondary process, and 'telling, following, understanding stories is simply the "continuation" of these untold stories' (1985, 75).

From the point of view of temporal experience, then, Ricoeur's circle seems to introduce a doubleness into the present, since the present is effectively prestructured by something we might normally think of as following from that experience: by the telling of the untold stories that we live by. In fact, Ricoeur's whole account of narrative is very closely bound up with the concept of doubling. We often find him talking about narrative emplotment as a kind of schism, a splitting in two, for the purposes of reflective judgement, as a result of some constitutive split that narrative possesses between utterance and statement:

> To introduce this distinction, it suffices to recall that the configuring act presiding over emplotment is a judicative act, involving a 'grasping together'. More precisely, this act belongs to the family of reflective judgements. We have been led to say therefore that to narrate a story is already to 'reflect upon' the event narrated. For this reason, narrative 'grasping together' carries with it the capacity of distancing itself from its own production and in this way dividing itself in two. (1985, 61)

He calls this 'teleological judgement', but if we are to take seriously the notion of the present as an untold story, we have to view this teleology, this looking back from an endpoint, as part of the present moment itself. Narration, in other words, involves a kind of reflective split in the present moment, between the event and a perspective of teleological retrospect on the event. Interestingly, however, this is not simply a split between the narration and the event narrated; it is also a capacity for self-distance that narrative carries within itself that allows narrative to reflect not only upon the narrated event, but also upon itself. At first sight it can seem as if Ricoeur is conflating two very different kinds of schism here – the schism of utterance and statement in the narrative on one hand, and the schism of self-reflection on the other – but on closer inspection what is really at stake is the co-operation between the first schism and the relation between narrative temporality and the time of life. The drift of Ricoeur's argument in this section of *Time and Narrative* is exactly to propose the co-dependence of these two schisms in the circle of mimesis:

> If it is within narrative itself that we must distinguish between utterance (discourse in Benveniste's terms) and statement (narrative in his vocabulary), then the problem becomes double. It involves, first, the relation between the time of the utterance and the time of the statement and, second, the relation between these two times and the time of life or action. (1985, 65)

The problem of doubling is thus doubled but, importantly, the first schism, which divides the narration of the event from the event narrated, is a component in the larger relation between narrative and life. Ricoeur's brilliant insight here is to link both of these schisms to the question of verbal tense. One might say that the relation between tense and temporal reference is rather loose at the best of times, on the grounds that it is easy to refer to the past or the future in the present tense. In the case of fictional narrative, the deployment of tenses is looser still. Fictional narrative characteristically employs the simple past tense, or the preterite, which 'loses its grammatical function of designating the past', since 'the narrated action does not, properly speaking, occur' (1985, 65). As Karl Simms puts it in his book on Ricoeur, 'verb tenses do not necessarily coincide with the division of time into the past, present and future: there is often a mismatch between statement and utterance when it comes to verbs':

> Ricoeur wants to claim that in narrative fiction there is *always* a mismatch between verbal utterance and the statement made thereby, or at least, the verb tenses always mean two things at once: they simultaneously mean that the narrative is taking place in the past of the narrator, and that the narrative is taking place in some sense in the real past of the reader. Although the work is fiction, it is still significant that in real time as well as in narrative time the events *have happened* rather than *are happening* or *will happen*, otherwise it would not be typical to use the past tense for narratives. (Simms 2003, 90–1)

This pretence, in fiction, that events are past in a way that is comparable to the pastness of events in real time, is one of the ways in which the process of mimesis passes from Mimesis 1 to Mimesis 2. It links the pastness of real time to what Ricoeur calls the 'as if' of fiction: 'it is *as if* the events of the narrative have happened in the past' (Simms 2003, 91).

We can easily extend this observation about tense, and therefore the importance of the mismatch that Ricoeur claims is always there in fictional narrative. It is true that events tensed in the preterite seem to be past for both the narrator and the reader, and this forges a link between fictional and real time, but in fact the differences that lie behind that similarity are more interesting. Put simply, events in the past have already happened but, in terms of the reading process, these events, despite being tensed as past, are at different times events that are happening or will happen. For a narrator, there is a kind of match because narrated events are all past in relation to the time of the utterance, but for the reader, events in the past are decoded as a kind of present, and indeed events in the past tense make up the future of the reading too. From the point of view of the process of reading, then, the mismatch between tense and time is quite profound, because fictional events can be both in the past and in the future, still to come, yet having already taken place. To read a narrative is to experience the present as if it were already past, and to know that the future is also already complete, and tensed in the past. One of the ways, then, in which the configuration of emplotment connects with the refiguration of the third stage of the mimetic circle is that the experience of real time becomes marked in advance by this mismatch between tense and temporal reference, and experienced as a story, in the past tense, while it takes place, and even in advance of its having taken place. This is part of what Ricoeur means when he talks about untold stories: that one of the effects of narrative in the circle of mimesis is to inflect the present, and even the future, with the retrospect of narrative teleology. When we read a narrative, we do not think of it simply as past. We decode it as a kind of presence, or make it present, and reciprocally, when we live our lives, we do the opposite, and think of the present as a kind of past, already complete in relation to some future point at which its untold story will be told, and in this reciprocity between presencing the past and retrospecting the present, the mimetic process forges the link between configuration and refiguration from the mismatch of tense and time. Ricoeur does not make this argument directly, but it does accord well with his remarks about the basic reflexivity of the narrative act. The narration of an event may itself belong to the family of reflective judgements, but we recognise here a mode of self-consciousness that operates outside of narrative, but which seems to draw on the resources of narrative: namely, the anticipation of retrospection that is necessarily involved when one thinks of oneself as a participant in a story still to be told.

In Ricoeur's argument, the link between Mimesis 2 and Mimesis 3 is not directly attributed to tense, but rather to other aspects of the manipulation of time in fictional narrative. Most notably, he talks about the relationship between utterance and statement as the distinction between narrating time and narrated time, the relationship that Genette refers to as duration. It is well known in narratology that the ratio of narrated time to the time of narration is highly variable in fiction, both between novels (from dynastic sagas to circadian fictions) and within novels (between sections of *To the Lighthouse*). This is, for Ricoeur, a ratio that is governed principally by the manipulations of narrative voice and point of view in fiction, since the present of narration can be attributed to the narrative voice, while the universe of narrated time is the discourse of characters, and admission to that universe is granted and withheld, dwelt upon or hastily summarised, by that narrative voice. These two categories, narrative voice, which answers the question 'who is speaking?', and point of view, which answers the question 'from where do we perceive what is shown to us?', provide Ricoeur with a more complex framework for temporal structure than the tense of the verb. These two metaphors, the visual and the audible in a universe in which nothing is seen or heard, succeed, Ricoeur thinks, where the category of tense fails, in situating the point of transition between configuration and refiguration, and marking the point of intersection between the world of the text and the world of the reader. My own view is that they represent an expansion of the category of tense to a level of discourse above the grammatical tense of the verb, and that their operations are necessarily part of what a tense narratology must explain.

We can draw some conclusions, then, about the kinds of answers that Ricoeur provides to the problems that an Aristotelian conception of mimesis brings to the dynamics of surprise. We can say, first, that an expanded conception of mimesis leads to an expanded conception of tense, linked to, but at a higher level of discourse than, the tense of the verb. We can say that the circle of mimesis in Ricoeur offers a framework for a kind of typology of surprise, more capable of answering the question 'whose surprise?'. We find in the circle of mimesis a hermeneutic circle between narrative and life which is also predicated on (an expanded sense of) the category of tense, and which also encompasses the metaphors of narrative voice and point of view while restoring them to their properly temporal predicament. Sternberg's sense that surprise in narrative is to be understood as unforeseen disclosures as much as unforeseeable events is also addressed by a narratology that sees voice and point of view as part of the temporal unfolding of a narrative. Ricoeur's account of tenses opens an enquiry into the relationship between narrative as, in itself, a reflection on a narrated event, and the topic of narrative reflexivity, as well as on the function of narrative in the cognitive entanglement of reading and living. We should add that the theory of surprise seems to have some trouble in detaching itself from the theory of literary value, with the affects of the unexpected either playing into the categories of Aristotle's complex and simple plots or drawing on the valorisation of novelty more generally. But most importantly, it takes us to the threshold of an observation about tense structure that Ricoeur does not quite formulate: that the narrative preterite, that signal of the entry into narrative, is a structure that, in the reading process, signifies the pastness of events even when they lie ahead, and so joins the unforeseeable future to the condition of its having already taken place in the narrative simulation of time.

A tense narratology must move beyond the straightforward opposition that presides over most plot typologies when it comes to the question of surprise, and which Sternberg expresses as a kind of inescapable trade-off:

> The gain of either strategy, or plot type, is the other's loss. Inevitably so, because you cannot have at once the jolt of the unforeseen and the juggernaut of the expected, the abrupt ('complex') regression from effect to cause and the tense, oppressive ('simple') progression from cause to effect. (1992, 484)

Why not? If the narrative preterite characteristically involves us in temporal structures in which futurity and completion can inhere in the same verbal forms, it follows that the jolt of the unforeseen and the juggernaut of the expected are possible in the same moment in narrative, joined together and yet distributed between different points of view or temporal locations. Perhaps we would be better to think of this apparent impossibility, of expecting and not expecting something in the same moment, as a foundational impossibility for narrative which derives from the more basic impossibility of a future that is already in place. This is not to say that there are no surprises in narrative, no unexpected or unforeseen events available to a reader, but rather an ontological gap between narrative sequences and lived temporal experiences. Does Derrida's account of the event, not an unforeseen occurrence but an unforeseeable one, ever apply in written narrative, given the accessibility and completion of the full sequence? It is towards this conceptual metalepsis, the conceptualisation of the future across the boundary between narrative and life, straddling as it does the gap between the unforeseen and the unforeseeable, that the cognitive and conceptual interrelation of narrative and lived experience can be analysed.

PART II
The Unpredictable and the Future Anterior

Chapter 3

Prediction and the Age of the Unknowable

There is the future that we can predict, and then there is the unexpected. In an obvious way, the unexpected is the failure of prediction, and in a less obvious way, it comes into view as a result of the success of prediction. Prominent unexpected events, such as 9/11, the tsunami in the Indian Ocean in 2004, the financial meltdown of 2008, are moments that highlight our everyday reliance upon and expertise in prediction. Expert prediction is what we hold to account in the event of the unexpected. In moments of catastrophe, in cases of child abuse and murder, for an unforeseen storm, there is always someone who should have seen the future coming. Even creative writing tutors were expected to have foreseen the unexpected in the Virginia Tech massacre in April 2007. Perhaps it is part of the same logical co-dependence that, in an age driven by financial forecasting, market research predictions, electoral polls, the actuarial sciences, climate change projections and widespread gambling – in an age of increasingly interested, detailed and accurate prediction, the notion of the unpredictable has emerged as a way of characterising the new epoch. The notion of unpredictability comes with a certain scientific credibility in the contemporary age, which derives from difficulties in the modelling or simulation of complex systems in biology: systems so fundamentally complex that their behaviour cannot be encapsulated in a formal model, and therefore cannot be predicted. The notion of complexity, and its incumbent problem of unpredictability, has been widely applied to the social sciences, and particularly the description of economic systems. Joshua Cooper Ramo is one of many commentators who have recently (since the economic crisis of 2008) popularised the notion and used it to characterise a range of problems in economic and political forecasting. Ramo's central metaphor is the sand pile: an experiment conducted in the late 1980s which demonstrated that, if you pile sand grain by grain until it forms a cone, the event of an avalanche in that pile is absolutely unpredictable. If there is some limited ability to describe the interaction of the first few grains, by the time the pile contains a thousand, it has already attained a level of complexity that defies prediction, and 'nothing in the history of physics or mathematics could tell you what was going to happen next' (2009, 53). For Ramo, the recognition of unpredictable complexity is an essential stage through which understanding has to pass in order to ensure that an analytical model is capable of adapting to the dynamics of complex systems, and every field of scientific study has its moment – 'Heisenberg injecting uncertainty into quantum physics, Alfred Tarski bringing unpredictability to mathematics, Kurt Gödel bringing incompleteness to logic, Benoit Mandelbrot doing the same for fluid dynamics and Gregory Chaitin for information theory' (Ramo 2009, 46) – has its moment of adaptation to the bewilderingly unknowable. It is, for Ramo, one easy step from the dynamic energy of the sand pile to the demand that we accept the fundamental unpredictability of the global order, and a condition of 'constant surprise'. A similar argument is found in Nassim Nicholas Taleb's notion of the 'Black Swan Event', which refers to a kind of logical falsification that comes about through the occurrence of an unexpected event. For Taleb, the notion of a black swan is rooted in Karl Popper's argument for the fallibility of inductive reasoning, which declares that the proposition 'all swans are white' requires the discovery of only one black swan for its falsification, however much this discovery lies outside the scope of sensible expectation. In this way, the 'discovery' of black swans in Australia in the eighteenth century acts as a falsification of the widespread belief, in seventeenth-century Europe, that 'all swans must be white', and is subsequently used by John Stuart Mill in the nineteenth century to refer to a species of logical falsification. Taleb's use of the Black Swan Event modifies this logical fallacy to describe high-impact historical events that are 'outliers' in relation to the 'realm of regular expectations' and which, because they are absolutely unpredictable in relation to past experience, are deemed impossible. The supposed impossibility of the unpredictable event is, however, subject to a process of revision which seeks to establish its predictability in retrospect, through the construction of explanations of its occurrence. The idea of a retrospective predictability is therefore offered as a characteristic human response to the unexpected event whereby the unexpected is reshaped by the teleology of narrative form in a demonstration that it had been predictable, sometimes even a pretence that it had been expected, all along.

The importance of the unexpected event for this idea of an age of the unpredictable can be broken down into several components. First there is a foundational link between the notion of unpredictability and a general preponderance of prediction in the world. Second, there is a tendency to draw upon the authority of the physical sciences, and on their predictive function, as a basis for understanding complex systems of a more social kind, in order to establish unpredictability as a general predicament shared by the physical and the social sciences. And third, there is a retroactive stage in which the unpredictable is folded back into a narrative that establishes the predictability of happenings by revision. There are two assumptions here that may require a little further reflection: that the complexity of a sand pile properly translates into the social complexity of a global economy or political order; and that the translation of the unpredicted into the predictable is usefully or properly thought of as narrativisation or, in Taleb's phrase, as the 'narrative fallacy'. These are assumptions taken up by Popper in his account of scientific discovery in general, and most directly in 'Prediction and Prophecy in the Social Sciences' (Popper 2002). For Popper, the idea that there is a general preponderance of prediction, like the idea that one of the tasks of the social sciences is the prediction of political developments or social revolutions, is based on a kind of slippage between one kind of prediction and another: what he calls conditional and unconditional prediction. In fact, Popper offers a rather muddled account of this distinction. Ordinary predictions in science are conditional, he argues, in that they 'assert that certain changes will be accompanied by other changes', as, for example, a change in temperature in water will be accompanied by the boiling of the water. An unconditional prediction may or may not be based in conditional predictions of this kind; a physician may, for example, predict that a patient with scarlet fever will develop a certain kind of rash on the grounds that when A happens, we can expect B, but we think of this as unconditional because of the absence of necessity, or because the degree of probability established by induction is lower than for the boiling of water. The problem with unconditional predictions is that, while they can seem to draw on ideas of necessity, or high degrees of probability established by the conditional predictions of theoretical sciences, they may also have no such basis. The predictions of what Popper calls *historicism* in the social sciences are not, in fact, based in conditional predictions at all, and could not be, since historical prophecies can be derived from scientific conditional predictions 'only if they apply to systems which can be described as well-isolated, stationary, and recurrent' (2002, 457) – systems which are very rare in nature, and 'modern society is surely not one of them'. If this distinction seems to suggest that it is unsafe to regard these two kinds of prediction in the same way, or allow the latter to borrow from the credibility of the former, it does not seem to destroy the negative version of the slippage – namely, that unpredictable systems are ubiquitous in nature – so that the unpredictability of such systems is analogous to the condition of historical prophecies. The distinction, in other words, does not take us forward from notions of simplicity and complexity, or prevent us from thinking of the economy as a sand pile. Philosophers are well acquainted with the idea that the value of a prediction is related to the level of its risk, to its specificity and detail, that there are safe predictions of little value, and risky ones that relate to high levels of uncertainty and complexity, and from this point of view, Popper's distinction offers little more than a scale that runs from the safe to unsafe inductions. It also offers no basis on which to distinguish, as he claims to do, between the authority of scientific prediction and the lack of authority in the historicisms of the social sciences, since both operate between the poles of an ordered system in which rational prediction is possible and a chaotic one in which prediction is difficult, and notions of the unpredictable and the unexpected remain perfectly transferable between the two domains. If we turn to the second assumption, that narrative has some role in the retrospective translation of the unpredictable into its opposite, in the backward movement of explanation, we also find Popper articulating a common precept. There exists, for Popper, a clear connection between prediction and narrative in the social sciences, in that he gives the name 'historicism' to the 'view that the story of mankind has a plot, and that if we can succeed in unravelling this plot, we shall hold the key to the future' (2002, 455). Again, we have recourse to established philosophical wisdom here, and to the idea that prediction is not prediction at all unless its rational basis is discernible in advance of the event it foretells: that the prediction whose value is discernible only in retrospect is worthless. Neither Taleb nor Popper takes issue with this wisdom. For Taleb, hindsight is part of the pretence that the unexpected was predictable all along, and for Popper, the analogy between history and plot is only relevant if we are able to predict that plot, and so to hold the key to the future. In these positions on the value of the relation of narrative to prediction it is possible to discern two distinct questions, the first of which assumes that retroactive explanation might possess some heuristic value through which prediction can be refined for next time, and the second, that anticipation, expectation and prediction in the unfolding experience of a plot might have some analogical relation to the unwritten future. The most fundamental questions that guide this enquiry derive from these two accounts of the relationship between narrative and prediction. What function do unexpected events in narrative have for our cognitive control of the future in general?

Epochal temporality

The notion of an age of unpredictability suggests an epochal temporality which is distinctly modern. The notion that an epoch can be characterised or defined in relation to some aspect of its experience of time seems over-ambitious on two counts, which result from two distinct ways in which the notion of epochal temporality is a temporal concept: an epoch is itself a temporal concept, a gargantuan unit of history which inflates the notion of a moment to its highest level of complexity; and an epoch is under-stood as having a defining experience or conception of temporality. In this double temporalisation there are two impossibilities and a problem: the impossibility of representing the totality of an epoch, the impossibility of reducing the collective experience of time in that epoch to something comprehensible, and the problem of using one temporal concept to define another, or, in its more familiar form, of being unable to stand outside of time in order to reflect upon it. However impossible and problematic, the notion of an epochal temporality is certainly well established, and it is arguable that periodisation is impossible without some version of this double structure which defines an age in terms of its temporality. It may be that there is no other kind of periodisation, and that when we ask what are the characteristics of a given epoch, we really ask for an account of its relation to time. Special problems arise for self-periodisation in this regard, for the attempt to specify the temporality of the present. If perio-disation is properly thought of as a kind of historicisation, predicated on historical distance between the describing subject and the described object, in self-periodisation, where that distance is abolished, the speci-fication of epochal characteristics becomes part of the historical self-consciousness of that epoch's inhabitants. The double temporalisation of epochal temporality is compounded when self-periodisation, or historical self-consciousness, is itself one of the characteristics of the temporality described, as it is widely held to be for the epoch of postmodernity.

In accounts of the postmodern, the notion of epochal temporality is pronounced, and assumes these compounded forms, in which the time (epoch) is defined by the experience and the concept of time (temporal-ity), one aspect of which is epochal self-reflection. But the epoch of postmodernity is not usually described as the age of the unexpected, nor its temporality generally associated with unexpected events. Postmodern culture is routinely associated with nostalgia, memory, pastiche, simula-tion, rewriting, recycling, repetition and recontextualisation by cultural commentators, so that the future-orientation of faculties such as expec-tation, prediction and anticipation are all but absent in the most influential accounts of postmodern temporality. There are, nevertheless, obvious ways in which these accounts are consonant with notions of unpredictability and unforeseeability, though not generally expressed in those terms. The cultural theory of the postmodern is notable for a recurring theme of blocked futurity, in which political possibility, innovation and novelty, originality and progress have, however absurdly, been decommissioned with the passing of modernity. Most of these arguments describe some effect of intensified capitalism, which has resulted in a kind of indifference to the future, or a dilation or distension of the present to the point that it colonises the past and future. Fredric Jameson's account of the centrality of nostalgia in postmodern epochal temporality is accompanied, for example, by the notion of a 'perpetual present', what Steven Connor calls a 'distension of the present by retrospection and anticipation' in the rolling archive of 'the represented past and the past of representation' (Connor 1999, 21), collapsing past and future into an intensified consumption of the moment. The notion of a blocked future is normally understood in relation to a lost sense of the present that was characteristic of modernity, when present moments were structured as future orientations, turned towards the new in an attitude described by Terry Eagleton as 'an empty excited openness which is in one sense already here, in another sense yet to come' (Eagleton 1986, 139). 'It is as though postmodernity had borrowed from the modern its capacity for breaking with the past', Connor comments, 'while losing all of its forward impulsion', and effect of 'amnesia combined with acedia, or future-fatigue' (Connor 1999, 21). A similar sense of a capitalist intensification inhabits the account of epochal temporality in Lyotard's discussion of fragmentation, of the breaking up of *grands récits*, with their progressive views of history, into the shards of little stories which no longer accumulate, in the postmodern condition, into collective futures. In most of these accounts, the power of an intensified capitalism to restructure temporality for our times is assisted by speed, and particularly speed-enhancing technologies, from the steady progress described by David Harvey in the travel speeds of boats and planes, to the infinite speed of electronic technology emphasised by Virilio and Baudrillard; the idea of waiting for a distant future to arrive is, first of all reduced in span, then abolished by the simultaneity of capitalism in its global phase. The notion of infinite speed as a condition of simultaneity also finds its way from Lacan's account of schizophrenia into the cultural theory of Deleuze and Guattari, and provides a model for Fredric Jameson's ontology of the present, where schizophrenia is understood as a linguistic disorder that collapses the linear separation of moments into the present, transforming the controlled admission of meanings in a sentence or sequence into the babble of simultaneity. For

Andreas Huyssen, it is technology that has transformed modern into contemporary temporality to the point where we no longer think of the future as the modernists did, as something that lies ahead, before or in front of us, but as something that seems to 'fold itself back into the past' (Huyssen 1995, 8). Perhaps the most strident and influential statement of the disappearing future is found in Fukuyama's account of the End of History (Fukuyama 1992), in the thesis that, with the end of Marxism and the arrival of global liberal democracy, the ideological evolution of humankind has reached an end, in its final form as secular free-market democracy. Derrida's critique of this argument – his injunction for the reappearance of Marx – is well known, but it is worth recalling the survey he offers of thinking which invokes endings, death or failed futurity as the characteristics of an epoch; the eschatological themes of the end of history, the end of Marxism, the end of philosophy and the ends of man were, for Derrida, 'our daily bread' in the 1950s, and the reappearance in the 1990s of what he called, in 1980, the 'apocalyptic tone in philosophy' is a 'tiresome anachronism' (Derrida 2006, 16). These notions of simultaneity, stasis, the perpetual present, the blocked future and the afterlife have always been powerful images in what can be thought of as, on the one hand, the politics of time and, on the other hand, the philosophy of time. In the politics of time, the notion of a static, perpetual present is the anathema of emancipation and progress, the enemy of possibility and change, and the idea of a blocked future tends to operate as a kind of imagery, borrowing from the language of apocalypse metaphors of death and endings for the description of a future-less-ness which is not actual, but stands in the place of some lack of progress towards particular ends. In the philosophy of time, the notion of the static, perpetual present is associated with the non-human time of eternity, the infinitely distended present seen only by God, or, in its more contemporary setting, the block universe of contemporary physics, which attempts to reject the ego-centricity of presence, and the tensed view of time on which it depends. A political imagery of stasis borrows from and blends with a philosophical view of time which is fundamentally non-human. We should also observe a tension, in the language of cultural theory, between the actual future, to which humans have no access, and the projected future, which is part of the present but turns towards the future in expectation, anticipation, prediction and so forth. Projected futures are, in Peter Osbourne's words, 'a central part of the existential structure of any present moment' (Osbourne 1999, 41), and cannot be banished by technology, capitalism or globalisation. From this point of view, the perpetual present is associated not with the non-human timescapes of eternity or the block universe, but with the inescapability of the present of time-consciousness, and with the notion that human access to the past and the future is confined to recollections and projections that structure the present moment, as described from St Augustine to the contemporary phenomenology of time. The absolute inaccessibility of the actual future, together with the necessary instalment of projected futures in the present, can make the notions of an unpredictable or an unexpected future look more consonant with the phenomenology of time than some of the formulations of cultural theory that blend the philosophy with the politics of time, or confuse the projected with the actual future.

The notion of the unexpected is, as a model for epochal temporality, on one hand, more future-orientated than predominant accounts of the contemporary as an age of repetition, nostalgia, archivisation and memory, and on the other, entirely continuous with accounts of the loss of positive futurity that have characterised the postmodern: the unexpected future is nevertheless a future, but its unpredictability is consistent with the political meaning of failed futurity as lack of progress towards a known goal. Two different orders of temporality are visible in the account offered above which correspond to the double temporalisation of the phrase 'epochal temporality', one which concerns the lived experience of the present, in which the present is intensified and infinitely dilated by processes of commodification, technological change and globalisation, and the other which reflects upon the temporality of the epoch from a distance. I suggested above that these two orders are in some way inseparable, since the reflection alters what is reflected upon, so that part of the lived temporality of an epoch is the way that it adopts a position of reflective distance from itself. In the philosophy of time, the suture of the reflection and the reflected is itself an essential feature of the structure of temporality. Bergson, for example, discusses the structure as 'memory of the present', a basic split in consciousness between perception and reflection that structures every living moment:

> Every moment of our life presents two aspects, it is actual and virtual, perception on one side and memory on the other. Each moment of life is split up as and when it is posited. Or rather it consists in this very splitting, for the present moment, always going forward, fleeting limit between the immediate past which is now no more and the immediate future which is not yet, would be a mere abstraction were it not the moving mirror which continually reflects perception as a memory. (Bergson 2002, 147)

The co-presence of perception and reflection is, paradoxically, a temporal structure, in which the reflection bears all the marks of a memory without the critical one of temporal posteriority:

And yet it does not present to us something which has been, but simply something which is; it advances *pari passu* with the perception which it reproduces. It is a recollection of the present moment in that actual moment itself. It is of the past in its form and of the present in its matter. It is a memory of the present. (Bergson 2002, 148)

In one sense it may be 'of the past in its form', in having the properties of retrospect, but in another sense, in order to be retrospective, this memory of the present is *of the future*. It is a little bit of the future installed in the present. It is not the actual future, but an envisaged, virtual future which is part of the present, experiencing the present moment as one that *will have been*, as something that *will have happened*. If we scale this up from the individual towards the collectivity of an epoch, we have a similar structure which is, similarly, a quasi-temporal self-reflection: a lived experience of the historical present which walks *pari passu* with its future memory.

This argument contains within it a kind of defence of the tensions and slippages between the political and the philosophical, and between the actual and the projected future which characterise epochal thinking. If the virtual future is quasi-temporal, in the sense that the future is envisaged rather than actual, a co-temporal part of the present rather than an actual future, any thinking about the present in the present must be a quasi-memory of this kind, a reflection on the present in the manner of an envisaged memory from within the present, and therefore a present possibility which structures the existential moment, whether personal or collective, split between a present perception on one side and a memory of the present on the other. The future, in other words, is a possibility which belongs to the present, confined by the inaccessibility of the actual future, like the structure of any existential moment, to virtuality, and condemned to wait for the actual future to arrive. In philosophical terms, this is what is designated by the unexpected: the difference between the memory of the present that we project in the present and the memory of the present that actually comes about, or between the future that we envisage and the future that actually arrives.

The already seen and the unforeseen

There are two positions that we have reached that help to define the importance of the unexpected as a project for narrative theory. The first is that the structure of self-consciousness is temporal, and reciprocally, that the lived experience of the present moment is self-conscious. The second is that the relationship between the virtual and the actual future is never completed in the present, so that the envisaged future of predictions, expectations and anticipations has to wait for the actual future to arrive. Bergson helps us to connect this first position with the second, in a way that is highly suggestive of the experience of reading a narrative, or any linguistic sequence. The memory of the present, which keeps step with a situation as it progresses is, for Bergson, an aspect of the 'already seen', the feeling that something is already known. 'Could we recognise what is being unrolled', he asks, 'if we did not know what is still rolled up? Are we not able to anticipate at least the following moment?' (148). His answer to this question is that, because present instants are not separate, because the instant that is about to come is already 'broken into' by the one that is now present, it follows that the instant to come must also fall within the faculty of the memory of the present. It is as if the reflective faculty, the one keeping pace with perception, is already there as an expectation, even before the perception of an instant has any content – the form of knowledge without the matter – and we live in this way, 'unceasingly, towards what is on the point of happening'. The future is at stake in the memory of the present in two ways, not only, as I have suggested, in the idea that the memory is *of the future*, located in an envisaged future which looks back upon the present, but also in the sense that we already know what we do not yet know:

> As I cannot predict what is going to happen, I quite realize that I do not know it; but I foresee that I am going to have known it, in the sense that I shall recognize it when I shall perceive it; and this recognition to come, which I feel inevitable on account of the rush of my faculty of recognizing, exercises in advance a retroactive effect on my present, placing me in the strange position of a person who feels he knows what he knows he does not know. (Bergson 2002, 148–9)

There is a slightly different kind of excursion into the future here, in the form of an expectation that future perceptions will be accompanied by the same memory of the present as present ones, and this expectation makes one feel that one knows what is to come even before the perceptual content has arrived. I do not know what is going to happen, but I will have known, or I will know what will have happened, and the confidence of this empty prediction, this future perfect disposition, tilts us towards what is on the point of happening. There is, in other words, a feeling that the unforeseeable has been already seen, which comes from the expectation that we will know it when we see it. This recognition to come is what Bergson calls a false recognition, and is not in itself the structure of interest, but the example he offers of this kind of tilt towards the future as a kind of self-consciousness opens a useful line of enquiry. Like Augustine's example of the recitation of a psalm in book XI of *Confessions*, Bergson finds his model for this experience of the memory of the present, as a feeling of the already seen, in the mechanical repetition of something we once knew by heart but had long forgotten: 'As we recognize each word the moment we pronounce it, we have a feeling that we possess it before pronouncing it; and yet we only get it back while we pronounce it' (2002, 149). The duplication of the present into perception and memory places us in this position, of a kind of doubleness which makes us act and watch, pronounce and recognise, simultaneously. Changing the metaphor, this state is, Bergson suggests, also like an actor, acting his part and beholding himself play:

> The more deeply he analyses his experience, the more he will split into two personages, one of which moves about the stage while the other sits and looks. On the one hand, he knows that he continues to be what he was, a self who thinks and acts comfortably to what the situation requires, a self inserted into real life and adapting to the free effort of the will; this is what his perception of the present assures him. But the memory of this present, which is equally there, makes him believe that he is repeating what has been said already, and so transforms him into an actor reciting his part. (149)

There are three stages of this argument: the first stage is the splitting of the moment into two personages, one who perceives and the other who remembers, or, if you prefer your schisms without temporality, one who acts and one who watches; the second stage is the temporal confusion that this split generates for the movement into the future, which makes the present seem like a repetition of something that has already been seen; and finally there is an oscillation which shows itself in this passage, between a feeling of freedom and a recognition of the predetermination of the script or part. It is not just that we split into two personages, and that this self-consciousness is fundamentally temporal, but also that the temporality of self-reflection offers us two standpoints from which to experience time, which occur together, the first of which implies our freedom, while the second 'converts us into automata', repeating parts and playing roles automatically. The schism of Bergson's memory of the present produces 'the singular state of mind of a person who believes he knows what is about to happen at the same time that he feels quite unable to predict it' (2002, 150).

Philosophers of time are wont to turn to some kind of written or otherwise predetermined sequence when they need an analogy for the *nunc movens* of temporal experience. Augustine's recitation of a psalm, Bergson's mechanical repetition of a text learned by heart, and Husserl's listening to a melody are all examples in which the dynamic between the already written and the experiential present are conveniently encoded. Such examples prompt the narrative theorist to consider whether the written narrative offers some kind of mental model for the experience that Bergson describes as a kind of paradox: the future which has been foreseen and yet cannot be predicted. But a written narrative, like a psalm or a tune, clearly imports into an understanding of temporality elements of predetermination, predestination and fate that cannot be uncritically assumed for the description of human time, since the 'now' of a reading moves forward into a future which is already there, unalterable by efforts of will. If we accept the reading of a narrative as a model of temporal experience it seems to represent human action in its most passive mode in relation to a future that is not open, the arrival of which we simply await. The future, in a written narrative, is accessible to us, as readers, in a way that seems to render it ontologically distinct from the open future of life: a false future which is, in fact, the past, since it is already written. It is accessible beyond the faculties of anticipation, expectation and prediction, and therefore open to visitations and excursions of which those faculties, imprisoned as they are in the present, are incapable. It may even be known to us, if we have read it before, if we have some foreknowledge, as Augustine has of his psalm, or Husserl of his melody, that is absolutely unavailable to us in the ineluctable present of human temporality. If a certain kind of enquiry seems to close down as a result of these differences, another line of thought also opens up, guided by two questions. The first is the question of what it is about the written narrative that seems to make sense of time, even to philosophers of the present instant, and how this relates to a temporal experience in which we both know and do not know what is going to happen. The second is a question about the function of narrative as a factor in our cognitive control of the future, which is to say, for the way that it modifies our faculties of anticipation, prediction and expectation in relation to a future which is absolutely inaccessible. We might regard narrative as part of our memory of the present, in the sense that it is one of the cognitive resources that we have at our disposal to anticipate what is to come, not only because we anticipate when we read, but perhaps more significantly because we anticipate in the mode of retrospect, as if we already know how to look back upon the present.

Chapter 4

What Will Have Happened: Writing and the Future Perfect

'I cannot predict what is going to happen', Bergson says, 'but I foresee that I am going to have known it.' This empty foresight offers a grammatical form, the future perfect, which links together the structure of an existential moment, the engagement with a fictional plot, and contemporary epochal self-consciousness. In 1977, Robert Champigny published a philosophical study of mystery stories titled *What Will Have Happened*, a tense form that creates a conjunction between a prospective present and the retrospective future. Speaking of the investigative sequence of a mystery story or detective fiction, what makes aesthetic sense for Champigny 'is that an investigative sequence can turn the opposition between narrative questions and answers into a tighter tension or complementarity between narrative progression and retrogression':

> This is implied in the phrase 'what will have happened'. Otherwise, the interplay between prospective and retrospective outlooks, predetermination and postdetermination would concern the reading process only. (Champigny 1977, 59)

This is an intriguing claim, partly because it seems to want to locate the interplay between narrative progression and retrogression not only in the temporality of a reading, but in the investigation itself: the structure of what will have happened is not only the structure of general future orientation, in reading or in life, but a particular kind of narrative – the investigative sequence – capable of binding prospect and retrospect together in an unusual complementarity. This is of interest not only because it repeats what Todorov famously claimed about the double time of detective fiction in 1966, but because it is otherwise surrounded by occasions, not generally well known, and of which Champigny's argument seems to know nothing, of invocations of the future perfect as a tense for our times: there is, for example, a strange flash of interest, in 1978, in the future perfect as a postmodern tense and temporal structure. The future perfect is the tense that expresses a future event which is anterior to another event ('I will have eaten breakfast by the time you get here') and is also known as the future anterior. The future anterior began its career in epochal description in the opening of Derrida's *De la grammatologie* in 1967, which refers to the incoming future, after the closure of our historico-metaphysical epoch, as 'that which guides our future anterior'. This idea, along with the one expressed in the previous sentence, of a future that 'breaks absolutely with constituted normality' and 'can only be proclaimed, *presented*, as a sort of monstrosity' (Derrida 1976, 5), seems to underlie the account of the postmodern epoch given by François Lyotard in 1978 under the title *What is Postmodernism?*:

> The artist and the writer, then, are working without rules in order to formulate the rules of what *will have been done*. Hence the fact that work and text have the characters of an *event*; hence also, they always come too late for their author, or, what amounts to the same thing, their being put into work, their realisation (*mise en oeuvre*) always begins too soon. *Post modern* would have to be understood according to the paradox of the future (*post*) anterior (*modo*). (Lyotard 1984, 62; original italics)

In the same year, Kristeva describes in 'Women's Time' a

> new social ensemble superior to that of the nation, within which the nation, far from losing its own traits, rediscovers and accentuates them in a strange temporality, in a kind of 'future perfect', where the most deeply repressed past gives a distinctive character to a logical and sociological distribution of the most modern type. (Kristeva 1981, 188–9)

In both arguments, the logic of the future perfect is a description of a break with the past, with what Derrida called 'constituted normality', which takes the form of a future projection rooted in a memory of the past, a protention founded in retention, and as such it reproduces for the epoch the structure of the lived existential moment. The future cannot be known, but its contentlessness is given form, like Bergson's expectation that he is going to have known it, by the strange temporality of what will have happened. There are also arguments that seek to establish the future anterior as a mode of experience in the present, not as a protention founded in retention so much as a retention embedded within a protention, which transforms the present into the object of a future memory. Christopher Bigsby makes this argument for the temporality of American culture:

> America has so successfully colonized the future that it has mastered the art of prospective nostalgia. Its natural tense is the future perfect. It looks

forward to a time when something will have happened. It is a place, too, where fact and fiction, myth and reality dance a curious gavotte. It is a society born out of its own imaginings. (Bigsby 2006, 1)

Bigsby's formulation takes its inspiration from the annual celebration of an event which has not yet, and never will happen: namely, the birth of Captain James Kirk, Captain of the Starship *Enterprise*, in Riverside, Iowa, and in this way it links the non-actuality of the future to the virtuality of fictional imaginings and accords to these imaginings an originary status for the society that begets them. We encounter this kind of thinking about cultural temporality, and the idea that fictional imaginings have some foundational role in this temporality, wherever we look because we have inherited them, through deconstruction, from the phenomenology of time. The incoming monstrosity that Derrida foresees in epochal terms, for example, can be found in the temporal paradoxes most closely associated with deconstruction's critique of the phenomenology of time-consciousness. The notion of the logic of supplementarity, for example, which Derrida develops from his early critiques of Husserl, is one of those strange structures, in which a future possibility seems to act as an origin – 'a possibility produces that to which it is said to be added on' – and this inversion of future and past, of possibility and cause, lies also behind Derrida's writings about archive fever, the archivisation of which 'produces as much as it records the event' (Derrida 1998, 17). Though the idea of the future perfect as such occurs only in flashes as a source of insight into epochal temporality, the anticipation of retrospection that the tense encodes can be seen as epochal to the extent that the anticipatory structures of the existential moment are reified by our archiving technologies, inscribed in our cultural imaginings and inherent in our self-periodisations.

Time will tell

The claim that the future perfect is a tense for our times, that it has some special power to describe temporal structures which are distinctly contemporary, can seem hyperbolic, especially since the anticipation of retrospection is central to the philosophical account of lived moments in general. It may be that there are new, technological, widespread and collective forms of self-consciousness that bring this temporal structure into the foreground as the structure of self-consciousness in general, but it is as rash and unhistorical to claim that we inhabit an age of the future perfect as it is to regard contemporary conditions as an age of unpredictability. Both of these notions, the future perfect and the unpredictable, nevertheless demonstrate a certain narrowness, a kind of exclusion, that took hold in the cultural theory of the postmodern, and continues to dominate in thinking about epochal temporality, which casts the present as indifference to the future. Lyotard and Kristeva, in 1978, show that questions of the future were installed alongside the problematics of recollection and repetition that dominated postmodern thought, with the kind of necessity that installs protention alongside retention in all thinking about time. But if these necessary, strategic emphases on the future were, in fact, guided by Derrida's invocation of the future anterior, there are two things that they left behind of Derrida's famous remarks in the 'Exergue' to *Of Grammatology*. In Derrida's remark, the new epoch, which cannot be foreseen, is the monstrosity that guides our future anterior, so that the future anterior is the relation with the unforeseeable itself, and not the characteristic of the epoch to come. The sense of the future anterior as unforeseeability is transposed in Lyotard and Kristeva into a paradox, a strange temporal logic 'of the most modern kind'. If there is a glimpse of this epochal monstrosity to come, for Derrida, it is the closure of an epoch of the phoneticisation of writing, and the opening of a science of writing, and this conjunction of the unforeseeable with writing is softened, if not lost, in the notion of the future perfect as a postmodern tense.

Though the future perfect and prediction are closely related, they are not the same thing. In the abstract, which is to say without specific context, they are both anticipations of the future which have to wait for their fulfilment or verification, but there is a subtle difference of location of the future position which is envisaged: where prediction imagines an event in the future (x will happen), the future perfect imagines a time further into the future in relation to which that future event is past (x will have happened). This question of the relationship between prediction and the future perfect is taken up by Geoffrey Bennington in 'Towards a Criticism of the Future', in the volume *Writing the Future*, published in 1990. This volume, which was based on a Warwick conference in 1986, is one of the rare places where the question of the future perfect is systematically explored not only as epochal temporality but also, more importantly, explored in the context of its original relation to what Derrida called writing. Bennington understands Derrida to be a philosopher who 'constantly writes about the future, *without making any predictions*' (Wood 1990, 19; original italics). In order to elaborate this structure, Bennington begins with Kant's *Prolegomena to any Future Metaphysics that will be able to Come Forward as Science*, in which Kant sets out not the future metaphysics itself but a prediction that such a metaphysics will be discovered. This kind of prediction, of what will be written, as opposed to what will have been written, writes for 'the future proper as against the future perfect, at least in so far as the future perfect has always already been contained in the past' (1990, 20). For Bennington, the future perfect is not a prediction, is not properly thought of as future time reference at all: 'future perfect because *perfectum*, complete already, and therefore not future at all' (1990, 20). There is a slippage away from the formula that I have just given (x will happen versus x will have happened) in Bennington's account into the view that because x will happen, it will already have happened, not only at some future time posterior to x but at the time of the utterance; for Bennington the future perfect seems to carry with it the logic of the always already, as if its completion in the future robs the future of its open and unpredictable character. It is not logically necessary to view the future perfect in this way. What will happen is distinguished from what will have happened, the future from the future perfect, by the addition of a second event in relation to which a first event is complete. Connotations of fate, repetition or the *always already* accrue to the future perfect only as a result of the tension between the uncertainty of prospect and the certainty of retrospect, but that retrospect is virtual, envisaged, predicted in tandem with the event concerned. To think otherwise would be to conflate the anticipation of retrospection with retrospection itself, or the virtual completion of the future perfect with the actual completion of the past tense. But it is exactly this tension, this possibility of confusion and conflation, which Bennington exploits for the description not only of the future, but for the conjunction of writing and the future. Speaking of Rousseau's fear, in the *Dialogues*, that his text might fall into the hands of his enemies, Bennington defines again the particular relation to the future entailed in the future perfect:

> This 'Histoire' explicitly addresses the two sorts of relation to the future we saw in Kant's *Prolegomena*: Rousseau writes that the 'Histoire' will tell 'what was [my text's] destination, and what has been its destiny': destination as projection to the future, destiny as the inevitable folding back of the future perfect. Or vice versa. I shall suggest that the drama and pathos involved in these texts are not to be read as symptoms of Rousseau's character or pathology, but as extreme indications of the structure of writing in general in its irreducible relation to the future, to both destination and destiny. (1990, 26)

The vice versa is important here. If it seemed, for a moment, as if destination named a projection into the future and destiny the folding back into the past of the future perfect, it is the interchangeability of these terms that characterises writing. In Rousseau's own words (embedded above), it is destiny that is joined to the *perfectum* of the past perfect (what has been its destiny), while destination is mere past (what was its destination). In Bennington's extrapolation, the structure of writing in general has an irreducible relation to both destination and destiny: that writing is both where we are going and where we will have been.

In this conception of writing, as the 'affirmation of that imbrication of destination and destiny' (1990, 28), Bennington couples prediction to the future perfect, or joins the future that we predict, desire or try to bring about with the one that actually arrives; he both insists on the distinction and joins the two entities inseparably in his account of writing, like the two sides of a sheet of paper. He does this with particular reference to the question of the addressee – the notion that a text has a particular destination in mind, but is vulnerable to the possibility that it will fall into other hands – and in so doing invokes a complex thematics of postcards, signatures, letters that go astray, apostrophes and addresses, telegrams and emails through which Derrida has linked the future and writing after *Of Grammatology*. But the presence of an addressee is not required for the association of writing and time suggested here, and the interaction between destination and destiny in writing can be understood more clearly without plunging into that particular sea of suggestivity, and following instead this unfolding relation of the future perfect to writing, particularly as it opens on to questions of fate and chance, destiny and freedom. There are particular examples of the future perfect which have attracted critical interest exactly for this imbrication of destination and destiny associated by Bennington with writing, and none is more striking than Mallarmé's use of the tense in 'A throw of the dice will never abolish chance', discussed by Jean-Michel Rabaté in the same volume. Mallarmé's 'most perfect of future perfects', as Rabaté describes it – 'Rien n'aura eu lieu que le lieu'; 'Nothing will have taken place but place' – differs from the empty prediction of what will have happened most obviously by being a negation, and this gives it a predictive content of radical scope. For Rabaté, the key indeterminacy that this future perfect presents is between the notion of place as the space of nature and the blank page of the poem, and this is the conflation performed by the poem as a whole:

> Mallarmé's future perfect has to be understood in the context of the movement towards the future which the 'law' of his poem enunciates: 'A throw of the dice will never abolish chance' ... The coupling of a 'never' with 'will' as future modalization still balancing between prediction and interdiction ... creates an orbit on which the future perfect stars will have been seen as a literary constellation. 'Nothing' takes up 'never' and is necessary to radicalize the negation, thereby stressing the undecidability of place; 'place' is both the space of nature and the blank page of the poem. (Rabaté 1990, 39)

Yes it is, but the primary ambiguity of place in 'nothing will have taken place but place' is the displacement of the temporal meaning of 'taken place' with the spatial meaning of 'place', and this is then followed by the undecidability of what place then means in this context. The constellation referred to here is part of a retraction that follows from the radicalised negation that nothing will have taken place: nothing 'except perhaps a constellation'. For this to have been seen as a literary constellation is a question of interpretation, a question of whether the future reader of the poem regards the taking place and the place of the poem as events in nature, or as the language and place of the poem itself. The idea of events in nature (the poem's shipwreck) taking place in a place (the sea, a deserted horizon) is inseparable, for Rabaté, from the idea of the poem itself, its words and its place on the page, and in this way the condition of writing is encoded as an analogue in the image it generates. The question of reading, of the future reader as the reception and interpretation of the poem, is also, for Rabaté, a kind of temporal tension between 'the presence of a page and the future of a writing seen on it' which corresponds (his word) to Mallarmé's much flouted conviction that 'un présent n'existe pas': 'What replaces, takes the place of a "présent" is the simple "avoir lieu" of the poem' (1990, 40). Rabaté's argument here seems constantly to escape him, lying as it does just beyond his powers of exposition, depending as it does on suggestion and metaphorical resonance – a kind of critical writing which, as he says himself of Mallarmé's criticism, is so strangely written that it looks like poetry. It is, as much critical writing is, a reprise of its object, and as such it is difficult to decide if the constellation he sets out – of events, writing and a certain view of time, in which the present is replaced by the future perfect, of what will or will not have happened – is the property of the poem or its reading. Either way, Mallarmé and Rabaté between them help to progress the enquiry into the future perfect beyond those mysterious and sweeping epochal pronouncements, and in the direction – a triangle of future time, writing and being – that I want to develop in relation to narrative.

Mallarmé's poem, according to Rabaté, is about a scene of cosmic disaster, in which 'an old master, God, the poet, a mathematician, has made one last effort at creation, but this effort is soon engulfed in a real or metaphorical shipwreck which spells the failure of art' (1990, 40), and it is this list of potential substitutions that allows him to move so freely between event as nature and as writing. If Rabaté reads the master as poet, and becomes himself the poet of the future perfect, a good candidate for its mathematician, for the person who elaborates the mathematics of the future perfect, is Alain Badiou, who devotes a chapter of

Being and Event to Mallarmé's poem. Badiou himself admits no rigid distinction between the poet and the mathematician, and this is one of the reasons that 'A Throw of the Dice' resonates for him as an allegory of all his favourite subjects, but it is particularly as a poetic formula for the event that Badiou explores the poem. The major project of *Being and Event* is to show that the structure of what he calls an event is most adequately described in the language of set theory, a structure that is divided between a present time in which the event is unpredictable, indiscernible and unnameable, and a future time, when it will have happened, from which it can be 'ontologised' and retroactively named as a part of the situation that it did not seem to belong to in the first place. Badiou effectively adds his name to the tradition of those who have connected the perfected modality of the perfect tense to the temporality of the detective novel when he confronts the enigma of Mallarmé's poem, or any of his poems: 'There is a certain element of the detective novel in the Mallarméan enigma: an empty salon, a vase, a dark sea – what crime, what catastrophe, what enormous misadventure, is indicated by these clues?' (Badiou 2006, 191). This kind of defunct event possesses a 'there-has-been' which must be reconstructed – a system of clues 'whose placement can be unified by one hypothesis alone as to what has happened'. But poetry is a special kind of language, because 'it trains language to the paradoxical function of maintaining that which – radically singular, pure action – would otherwise fall back into the nullity of place' (2006, 192). Though we have cast him as the mathematician of the future perfect, we can immediately see here the same mingling of his own language with Mallarmé's that generated some ambiguity in Rabaté's reading, as the opposition in Mallarmé's 'taking place' and 'place' resonates in this one between action and the nullity of place. I said above that Badiou finds in Mallarmé's poem an allegory for all his favourite subjects, and, since allegory distributes meaning ambiguously between literary language and its interpretation, it is the figure of allegory that authorises this blend of the language of a theoretical system and the language of the poem at hand. Hence, the situation presented in 'A Throw of the Dice' is, for Badiou, the metaphor of all evental-sites, and 'the paradox of an evental-site is that it can only be recognized on the basis of what it does not present in the situation in which it is presented' (2006, 192). The structure of an event, in the absence, yet, of that retroactive ontologising moment, involves some kind of projection towards that future moment in the form of a decision or a wager, and in this structure, poetry, and this poem in particular, have a special role: 'Poetry is the stellar assumption of that pure undecidable, against a background of nothingness, that is an action of which one can only know whether it has taken place inasmuch as one *bets* upon its truth' (2006, 192; original italics). Poetry in general has this structure of an event which must wait to know if it has taken place, and this poem in particular describes that structure of poetry in general, and by extension the evental-site in general, and in this way the poem's shipwreck is allegorised into self-commentary, as well as commentary upon the larger entities – poetry, events – to which it belongs:

> Why is the event . . . a cast of the dice here? Because this gesture symbolises the event in general; that is, that which is purely hazardous, and which cannot be inferred from the situation, yet which is nevertheless a fixed multiple, a number, that nothing can modify once it has laid out the sum – 'refolded the division' – of its visible faces. A cast of dice joins the emblem of chance to that of necessity, the erratic multiple of the event to the retroaction of the count. The event in question in A Cast of Dice . . . is therefore that of the production of an absolute symbol of the event. The stakes of casting the dice 'from the bottom of a shipwreck' are those of making an event out of the thought of the event. (2006, 193)

This structure, which joins chance to necessity and the presence of a situation to the retroaction of 'the count' (the counting of the number thrown, and the ontologising moment of what Badiou calls the count-as-one of a multiplicity), is a future perfect structure, and as such, it looks forward to a future which will have taken place, the content of which cannot yet be known. For this reason, the essence of the event cannot have 'any other form than indecision', and this is exactly what Mallarmé's image, of an arm coming out of the sea, hesitating eternally as he prepares to throw the dice, presents: an event in which the essence of the event is, in fact, lost – 'to play the round' and 'not to open his hand':

> In the first case, the essence of the event is lost because it is *decided* in an anticipatory manner that it will happen. In the second case, its essence is also lost, because 'nothing will have taken place but place'. Between the cancellation of the event by the reality of its visible belonging to the situation and the cancellation of the event by its total invisibility, the only representable figure of the concept of the event is the staging of its undecidability. (2006, 193–4)

If Rabaté's critical writing presents a kind of reprise of his poetic object, a more outlandish narcissism of ideas is at work when Badiou reads Mallarmé, as he translates him, with the assurance of a mathematician $(x = y)$, into an allegory of himself. As a result, the future anterior structure of the event as an inaccessible finality comes into view with great clarity:

The fixity of the event as result – its count-as-one – is carefully detailed by Mallarmé: it would come to *existence* ('might it have existed other than as hallucination'), it would be enclosed within its *limits* ('might it have begun and might it have ended'), having emerged amidst its own disappearance ('welling up as denied'), and having closed itself within its own appearance ('closed when shown'), it would be *multiple* ('might it have been counted'); yet it would also be *counted as one* ('evidence of the sum however little a one'). (2006, 196)

There is less of the ambiguity here than in Rabaté's reading about whether an idea belongs to the literary object or the critical subject. We feel the poem here being unambiguously marshalled into the service of Badiou's account of eventhood. But we might also agree with Christopher Norris in finding this acceptable, or more acceptable at least than other literary readings in *Being and Event*, on the grounds that

> the poetry is itself preoccupied – both thematically and by formal implication – with that whole intricate complex of ideas around chance and necessity, being and event or the emergence of the radically new from pre-existent modes of thought, whether these take the form of discoveries in mathematics or truly 'breakthrough' developments in the creative arts. (Norris 2009, 116)

Mallarmé's philosophical poem is, in other words, about being and the event, and it stands therefore as an emblem of the temporal structure of an event, as a future perfect whose content will emerge only later: an unpredictable happening which appears as it disappears, and must wait on the retroaction of the count-as-one to come into existence. There is, from this point of view, no great chasm between Mallarmé's vocabulary and Badiou's that would prevent this kind of movement between philosophy and poetry, and we can hear Mallarmé in the opening arguments of *Being and Event*: 'a situation is the place of taking place' (2006, 24). It is perhaps, then, to be expected that Badiou sees in Mallarmé's concluding maxim – Every thought emits a throw of the dice – a translation of his own – Decide from the standpoint of the undecidable, a conclusion that must not lead to nihilism, since 'if the event is erratic, and if, from the standpoint of situations, one cannot decide whether it exists or not, it is given to us to bet' (2006, 198).

We have moved from the idea that the contemporary world might, through some preponderance of successful prediction, be characterised by those events that are nevertheless unpredictable, to a philosophical notion of the event as absolutely unpredictable and an encumbent notion of human action as a kind of wager on the content of the future perfect, the what-will-have-happened. Like Taleb's black swan, Badiou's event is absolutely unpredictable, and like the black swan, it has a subsequent retroactive moment, thought of by Taleb as a narrative fallacy, and by Badiou as the foreclosing of the event from the outside by ontology. But whereas, for Taleb, there is a straightforward opposition of the truth of unpredictability and the deception of narrative retrospect, Badiou's notion of the truth-event is a kind of temporal loop of prospection and retrospection, takes the future anterior as the specific temporality of truth procedures, which is to say truths which are not static but rather which are procedures that span the temporal gap between a situation and the count-as-one. Christopher Norris identifies this will-have-been of the future perfect as the key structure which Badiou borrows from Cohen's account of how mathematical advances come about, and Žižek poses the question of whether the structure is that of ideology in general: 'Is not the identity of the Truth-Event and ideology further confirmed by *futur antérieur* as the specific temporality of generic procedures?' (Žižek 2000, 144; original italics). Perhaps, though, there is more direct line from Badiou and Žižek back to Lacan, and to one particular sentence in the *Ecrits* which identifies the future anterior as the tense of temporal becoming in general:

> I identify myself in language, but only by losing myself in it as an object. What is realised in my history is neither the past definite as what was, since it is no more, nor even the perfect as what has been in what I am, but the future anterior as what I will have been, given what I am in the process of becoming. (Lacan 2007, 247)

In the process of finding himself in language, Lacan loses himself in the gap between prospect and retrospect, and the future anterior is the name of the chasm into which he disappears.

If we add up the sum of these arguments, the future anterior has functioned as an account of the structure of the existential moment, the specific temporality of postmodernity, as the link of this temporality to the question of writing, as the emblem of the event in general, the grammar of change, the structure of ideology, and the tense of temporal becoming, and this before we have returned to the claim that written narrative also partakes of this strange mix between destination and destiny, between waiting for things to happen and their already having taken place. How, then, do we connect this apparently limitless philosophical and sociological scope of the future anterior with the innocent *will-have-happened* of narrative structure? The next chapter pursues an answer to this question by exploring the notion that the unexpected and the future anterior are, if not the same structure, secret sharers in any philosophical conception of temporality.

Chapter 5

The Untimely and the Messianic

Unexpected events, by standing out against the backdrop of routine and predictable moments, can make us see the originality of every moment, the novelty and unexpectedness of the present in general. Time, says Elizabeth Grosz, is 'a kind of evanescence that appears only at those moments when our expectations are (positively or negatively) surprised' (Grosz 2004, 5). This is not, for Grosz, the usual cliché, where a sensation to which we are normally dead comes into being as the defamiliarising effect of the unexpected, or the power of now elevates special people above the mundane. The unexpected, or the 'untimely', as she prefers it, is a strand in scientific and philosophical thinking, in Darwin, Nietzsche and Bergson (who she writes about at length), but also in Derrida and Deleuze (who she does not), that seeks to account for change through interruptions in the continuity of time, disruptions of our expectations, or unpredictable emergences in the physical universe. Within this strand of thinking Darwin's account of evolution has a special place, both for its recognition of the accidental, the random and the unexpected in the descent of life and for the introduction of those values into the methodologies of study formerly devoted to the pursuit of stable, predictive laws:

> In recognizing the surprising, unpredictable, and mobile force of time on the emergence and development of the multitude of forms of life, Darwin brings the concept of the *event* to the sciences. Events are ruptures, nicks, which flow from causal connections in the past but which, in their unique combinations and consequences, generate unpredictability and effect sometimes subtle but wide-ranging, unforeseeable transformations in the present and future. (2004, 8; her italics)

The evolutionary sciences are to be distinguished, from this point of view, from those other sciences, like physics and chemistry, which seek predictable regularity, just as the philosophies of Nietzsche and Bergson, which emphasise the open-ended and unpredictable nature of becoming, can be distinguished from philosophies of being in the present. The future, in these strands of thinking, 'is a gamble, like Nietzsche's throw of the dice, or an accident, like Darwin's natural selection' (2004, 12); it is 'a kind of leap or rupture' and 'an unexpected shift, the shift produced by the unexpectedness of events' (2004, 258).

The untimely, thus described, depends no less on retrospect than the predictable to come into view:

> Like all modes of historical interpretation or analysis, Darwinian evolutionary theory is fundamentally retrospective or reconstructive: given what exists now, we may be able to provide conjectured links that describe the temporal path to the present. But at a given moment in this history, it is impossible to predict what will follow, what will befall a particular trend or direction, let alone a particular individual, what will emerge from a particular encounter, how natural selection will effect individual variation, until it has occurred, until it is completed, or provisionally arrested. (2004, 8)

If Darwin introduced the concept of the event into the sciences, it is a concept with the same deferred structure that we found earlier in Badiou, of an unpredictable happening that must wait on a retroactive ontologising moment to come into being, but at any given moment in the sequence concerned, the predicament is one of indecision, and action has the character of a gamble. This is all very well for modes of historical analysis, but it tells us nothing interesting (beyond the obvious) about time (that we have to wait for retrospect), and seems empty from the point of view of any political programme for action. But this is just what Grosz, like Badiou, wants to do with this structure: bring a philosophical account of time, which is also a description of the temporality of the physical universe, to bear on political action. Can this be anything other than a programme for indecision or a gambler's charter? Is the description of cultural emergence, like the description of biological emergence, by being confined to retrospect, irrelevant to the question of how to act?

Often, when Grosz frames this question, the formulation is ambiguous between the explanation and the production of change, or between retrospect and action, and this in itself may be grounded in the view that action is informed and refined by retroactive explanation. So, for example, in the discussion of Darwin, the interest is in how the account of evolution might 'explain or limit cultural life and provide us with more complex ways of understanding politics and political change' (2004, 20). More specifically, Grosz finds in *On the Origin of Species* an extended expression of the link between biological and cultural emergence in Darwin's well-developed analogy of the history of languages to explain biological descent, 'a sustained homology between natural history and philology'. Again it is difficult to decide whether Grosz regards this analogy as one that compares species and languages, or natural history and philology:

> What species and languages share is a reliance on the concept of genealogy. Both are fundamentally temporal processes, capable only of retrospective rather than prospective analysis, which involve the hypothetical reconstruction of the past that has left only fragmented and decaying traces or remnants, modes in which order, timing, and precedence are irreducible factors, in which historicity and the movement forward of time are necessary conditions. (2004, 27)

We cannot think that life itself relies on a concept of genealogy, since life evolved without concepts, or that non-human species are capable of hypothetical reconstructions of the past. We are talking about the human understanding of these processes, not the processes themselves, and the prospective analysis that lies beyond our capabilities must be concerned with the predictability of linguistic emergence by the philologist, and not the genealogical systems of pedigree, filiation or inheritance that operate in the descent of languages. It is necessary to pose this question because it bears directly on the relation of retrospect and the unpredictable, but also because it presides over the question of the applicability of a category borrowed from the retrospective science of evolution to political action, not only because one is fundamentally retrospective and the other prospective, but also because politics is predicated on a degree of human agency to which evolution is indifferent. The confusion of the process itself with the explanation of the process, or of the object of analysis with the analysis itself, subtly projects the temporal properties of an explanation on to the process to be explained or lived, inflecting retrospect with anticipation and vice versa. The question we need to pose here is whether key temporal terms, such as *event*, *unpredictable*, *unforeseeable*, *retrospective* and *surprising*, are words that refer to an experience within a horizon of meaning, or an experience as constituting a horizon of meaning. Or, to strip the problem of its Heideggerian garb, we need to ask what *unpredictable* means that *unpredicted* does not, given that it refers to a property of an event that can come into view only after the event.

The political version of this problem is most visible in Grosz's conclusions, addressed first to the question of knowledge and then to the question of action. After the body of her argument, which moves brilliantly from Darwin to Nietzsche, before tracing the influence of evolutionary theory in Bergson, the project turns to this critical link between the understanding of time and the conduct of political action: the 'reconceptualization of time as continuity, as the order of transformation and change, as the condition of emergence and the active force of complication may provide a different angle from which to engage in political and cultural analysis and action' (2004, 252). The future, as we have seen, erupts, for Grosz, through a kind of leap or rupture, as an eruption of the untimely and not as the predictable, foreseeable continuation of the past, and this conceptualisation of surprise seems to have a special place in politics too:

> This leap *is* politics as much as it characterizes life. Politics is not reducible to this leap, it *is* this leap: recognizing itself in the past that prepares it, all politics, from the conservative to the radical, aims to develop a future through some efforts of the present. The conservative aims to present this future as the logical development on and progress of the past, shepherded by the self-interest of the present. A radical line, depending on its degree of radicality, more or less accepts as desirable a dislocation or incoherence between the present and the future. The future as surprise is welcomed with more or less anxiety or openness. (2004, 258)

It is difficult to see exactly what relation is being forged here between politics and surprise. This is partly because the conception of surprise oscillates, in these sentences, between the notion of a spontaneous emergence on one hand and an understanding or interpretation of events on the other, but there are also some unintelligible relations between the container and the contained, the universal set and its subsets. The leap of the untimely *is* politics, and yet only radical politics is characterised as a dislocation; all politics aims to develop a future through efforts in the present, but the future as surprise is welcomed passively as an emergence rather than as the production of those efforts. It is worth noting too the number of temporal relations at work in the formulation: that politics is an effort in the present that sees itself in the past, and develops a future, that the conservative presents a continuity (an understanding of events) between past and future via the present, and the radical accepts dislocation (a spontaneous emergence) between the present and the future, and finally that the response to the future as surprise is either anxiety or openness. We simply cannot tell whether the 'future as surprise' is a projection into the future in the present, as an envisaged surprise, or an act of retrospection, in which the unexpectedness of a future can be perceived in a former present, or a way of saying that the future arrives in the present as a surprise. Grosz, who has been so articulate in the description of untimely structures in the metaphysical understanding of time, often seems to emerge from these complexities in the political sphere with nothing more than a sense of the natural opacity of the future. 'Political struggle', she says at the end of her book, 'is directed, at its best, to a future we cannot directly recognize . . . and may not understand or control' (2004, 260).

It is interesting to note Terry Eagleton's account of Marx on this question of futurity and emancipation. Addressing an established misunderstanding that Marxism is a foolish dream of a perfect society without competition or inequality, Eagleton points out that the Jews were traditionally forbidden to foretell the future, and that Marx, the secular Jew, is 'mostly silent on what might lie ahead' (Eagleton 2011, 67). If anything, the practice of foretelling the future is an enterprise embedded in corporate capitalism rather than a legacy of Marx:

> The true soothsayers of our time are not hairy, howling outcasts luridly foretelling the death of capitalism, but the experts hired by the transnational corporations to peer into the entrails of the system and assure its rulers that their profits are safe for another ten years. The prophet, by contrast, is not a clairvoyant at all. It is a mistake to believe that the biblical prophets sought to predict the future. Rather, the prophet denounces the greed, corruption and power-mongering of the present, warning us that unless we change our ways we might well not have a future at all. Marx was a prophet, not a fortune-teller. (2011, 66–7)

In fact, the whole notion of history as a steady improvement emerged, rather, from an eighteenth-century Enlightenment 'hardly renowned for its revolutionary socialism'. Like Grosz's conservative, Eagleton's capitalist often holds an 'evolutionist' view of the future 'which regards it as simply more of the present' or as the 'present writ large', but where the inverted commas signify exactly the mistaken notion of evolution that Grosz's account of Darwin does so much to repair. For Eagleton too, surprise is exactly the force that will disrupt the complacent view of history as repetition of the same:

> This, by and large, is the way that our rulers like to view the future – as better than the present, but comfortably continuous with it. Disagreeable surprises will be kept to the minimum. There will be no traumas or cataclysms, just a steady improvement on what we have already. This view was known until recently as the End of History, before radical Islamists inconveniently broke History open again. You might also call it the goldfish theory of history, given that it dreams of an existence which is secure and monotonous, as the life of a goldfish appears to be. It pays for its freedom from dramatic shake-ups in the coinage of utter tedium. It thus fails to see that, though the future may turn out to be a great deal worse than the present, the one thing sure about it is that it will be very different. One reason why the financial markets blew up a few years ago was because they relied on models that assumed the future would be very like the present. (2011, 72–3)

If what we have been observing in Grosz is a difficulty in moving from readings in the metaphysics of time to a plausible account of political action, we see here in Eagleton a similar account of the issue about futurity in political action unencumbered by metaphysics. There are a few remarks in Eagleton's discussion about the non-existence of the future, and some observations about the open and yet limited potential that inheres in present moments, but not to the extent that any question arises about the translation of metaphysical to political questions. 'Emancipatory politics', Eagleton says, 'inserts the thin end of the wedge of the future into the heart of the present' and in so doing effectively describes the intersection of the present and future, without excess metaphysical baggage.

Derrida's discussion of time in the context of Marx, by contrast, emerges directly from his engagements with Kant and Hegel, Husserl, Heidegger and Levinas on metaphysical and ontological questions addressed to the nature of time. But the relationship between metaphysics and history is of interest not because metaphysics provides some basis on which to conceive political action; we need, rather, to be wary of a metaphysical concept of history. There is, of course, a very well-known passage from Derrida's *Positions* in which he outlines 'an entire system of implications' in the metaphysical concept of history, and particularly a well-known list that happens in parenthesis '(teleology, eschatology, elevating and interiorizing accumulation of meaning, a certain concept of continuity, of truth, etc.)' (Derrida 1981, 57). The statement was well known for its relevance in another context: namely, a kind of obsession in the early 1970s about the position of history in deconstruction, coming in the first place from European Marxism and later from an academy in the US obsessed with the opposition of formalism and historicism in literary studies. It was a refrain in both contexts that a rejection of history in Derrida's work was paramount to political quietism. But there has been a significant rethinking of Derrida since the publication of *Specters of Marx* in 1993, not only because that text addresses itself directly to Marx but also for a certain change in vocabulary, a shift away from a lexicon which, in the eyes of the overhasty, belonged to quietism (of deferral, lateness, delay and postponement), towards the language of action, or urgency and singularity, 'of promise, engagement, injunction and response to the injunction, and so forth' (2006, 37). There are two significant movements in the revision of Derrida, one which works backwards to discover, in the early writings, a set of interventions in the philosophy of time that lend themselves directly to the notion of disjunction and discontinuity, and another which recognises an increasing emphasis in Derrida on the notion of an unforeseeable future, on its untimely and transformative possibilities, and on the question of surprise.

There are many straightforward ways in which the early writings of Derrida can be rescued from those distorting contexts of his early reception, but we particularly need to focus on the question of the arrival of the unknown, of the as yet unthought, or the unexpected, to do justice to his interventions in the philosophy of time and history. One commentator who has shown this with brilliant clarity is Joanna Hodge in *Derrida on Time*. Hodge's demonstration is that the early writings on Husserl are deeply bound up with the question of the arrival of the unknown, just as his later writings, which seem to have left Husserl behind, can be seen as continued grapplings with the questions of transcendental phenomenology. So, for example, the question of the horizon and the event that we met in the first two chapters of this book, the idea of the horizon as an empirical basis for the metaphorics of the future, and of the event as something that comes from above, is one that comes directly from Husserl's attempts to allow for the arrival of the unknown:

> An empirical notion of the horizon precludes the arrival of the unknown, as Derrida supposes, but a transcendental conception of the horizon is not bound up to the metaphorics of visibility, invisibility and pre-visibility, and is not inscribed within a naturalised conception of time. (Hodge 2007, 31)

This is significant most of all because it is the gesture that links Husserl's notion of a transcendental (as opposed to empirical) horizon to Derrida's account of *différance*. Whereas, Hodge argues, the metaphors of visibility, invisibility and pre-visibility reduce time to spatialisation, the term *différance* is both temporal and spatial, and allows us to think about the emergence or arrival of the unexpected in ways that are not well provided for by the purely spatial, empirical horizon. Hodge claims that the problem of the arrival of the unknown in fact derives from Husserl's problem of the historical *apriori*: that is, the problem of how something becomes thinkable for the first time in history. This moment, which Husserl calls the *Erstmaligkeit*, is the instant that something unthinkable or unknown comes into view, and subsequently acquires the properties of an omni-temporality: that is, of being present at all times. It is therefore, from the point of view of the flow of time, something that emerges only at a particular point, but from the point of view of an untensed, or spatial view of time, a possibility that was present all along, omnipresent, and predating the time of its empirical emergence. We can see, in this paradoxical view of time, in the inseparable intertwining of empirical and transcendental horizons, the structure of supplementarity, formulated at the beginning of Derrida's career as the strange temporal structure that underlies so many of deconstruction's most controversial interventions: 'a possibility produces that to which it is said to be added on.' According to this strange logic, formulated in the early 1960s in Derrida's first published engagements with Husserl, there is a doubleness in temporal logic which makes *apriori* emergences, unforeseen events, surprises or supplements also part of a different temporal perspective in which, having emerged as a possibility, an event also takes its place before the origin to produce that to which it is said to be added on. *Possibility* almost always carries this meaning in Derrida, of a kind of conceptual pre-condition without regard for the temporal sequence in which it emerged. 'Pursuing this line of argument', Hodge argues,

> requires a transformation of Derrida's own notion of *différance*, from one apparently opposed to Husserl's horizontality, to one which, through the disruptions of the thinking of the future, as the *a-venir*, become a retrieval and deepening, indeed a rebirth of Husserl's thinking of the horizon and of the historical *apriori*. (Hodge 2007, 31)

As soon as the empirical and the transcendental horizon are allowed to mingle in this way, many of the intuitive approaches we have to thinking about time, which Hodge refers to above as 'a naturalised conception of time', are altered or corrupted. But so too are the tidy distinctions that Husserl depends on for his account of intention. Though Hodge is working hard, at this point in her argument, to construct an alliance between Derrida and Husserl, much of her book is a commentary on Derrida's basic unravelling of those distinctions. One such distinction is the opposition between static and genetic phenomenology: that is, the study of time from the point of view of a living present (static) as opposed to the point of time as an interaction of retention and protention, or the present as constituted by traces of the past and projections forwards to the future, of memory and expectation (genetic). This particular opposition is relevant to our thinking about narrative temporality for two reasons, the first of which is that it seems to rely on a further opposition, between time flow and time structure which we have been tracing in different ways in the experience of reading, and the second of which is that it points directly to an explanation of the importance of the unexpected in Derrida's thought. In effect, all of these oppositions – time and space, the empirical and the transcendental horizon, genetic and static phenomenology, time flow and time structure – operate together in Husserl as connected distinctions that 'permit the production of all exactitude', and in each case, Derrida argues, the preferred term cannot be kept separate from its opposite, and the preferences that Derrida perceives to be at work in Husserl are also the explanation for what might be thought of as a strategic counter-preference for that opposite. Hodge explains the strategy in the following way:

> The contrast [of these connected distinctions] is between a continuous temporality, connecting present impression, protention, and retention, which Husserl calls primary memory, and the discontinuity bridged in secondary memory. However, Derrida's critique identifies how for Husserl the difference between these two must present itself as a primordial impression, given in a continuous present of the living present, thus subordinating discontinuity to continuity. For Kant and for Husserl continuous time is the more basic; for Levinas and for Derrida discontinuous time, or interruption, is the more basic. (2007, 35)

Here, then, is a statement of some importance for the place of discontinuity, interruption and the unexpected in Derrida's writing: given the difficulty in unravelling structural and genetic accounts of time, or flow from structure, it becomes impossible to set one aside in favour of the other. Instead, we have to think about the two together, and to decide which is more basic. Derrida and Levinas differ from Kant and Husserl in valuing interruption over horizontality, secondary memory over primary memory, discontinuity over continuity and the unexpected over anticipation. For an argument interested in the interaction of time flow and retrospect, of the kind that we have observed in the reading process, there is no need to follow this demonstration of Derrida's interruption of Husserl in any more detail, but it is worth pointing to one of the issues that arises in Hodge's discussion of these connected distinctions: namely, the relationship between the naturalised time that Husserl seems to understand as a spatialisation based on an empirical horizon, and the tense structures of verbs. This naturalised time, and its ordinary conception of the future as that which lies ahead, previsible on a horizon, not only is the model that Derrida seeks to diverge from, but is also the ordinary view of time that underlies verb tense:

> In place of the threefold structure of time, as past, present and future, as given in natural time and in the tense structures of modern European verb conjugations, an alternate account of time begins to arrive. This 'other time' is at variance with the tense structures of the languages in which Derrida and Husserl write; and this poses huge problems for its expression and articulation within the grammars of natural language. (Hodge 2007, 39)

This is obviously a significant problem, that the verbs forms of natural language project into our understanding a notion of natural time, or what Heidegger calls an ordinary conception of time which encompasses assumptions that time is a series of *nows*, arranged in a line or a circle. The 'other time' is difficult to understand and express, going as it does against the grain of our verb forms, but it accompanies the ordinary conception of time like a secret sharer. This 'other time' is a conception that might be better adapted to address the transcendental horizon, or the concept of time that does not simply fit into the metaphorics of vision, and the concept of the future that does not simply regard it as that which is ahead. Hodge makes two suggestions that emerge from these arguments about the tendency of verb forms to naturalise time and the misfit between verb tenses and a more complex, transcendental time. The first is that, in Derrida's early work, the notion of writing, of *écriture* or arche-writing, is a practice based in this idea of a secret sharer or a contraband in natural languages: 'An arch-writing, *écriture*, is not thus constrained by natural tense structure, and thus cannot be transposed into the linguistic forms governed by natural tense structures' (2007, 39). The second is that this whole relationship between the natural and the transcendental, where the former is something embedded in natural languages and the latter is available only to the phenomenologist, is repeatedly placed in question by Derrida:

> He questions whether Husserl can be granted the presumption that natural languages tend at the limit to realise or accommodate themselves to the pure form of grammar, or the form of a transcendental logic, and whether the pure form of transcendental meaning or pure grammar can be kept secure from the naturalisations and localisations imposed by particular natural languages. (2007, 39)

Derrida prefers to think, according to Hodge, that these two grammars, the one that we use for our verb tenses in natural language, and the one that we use to describe transcendental time structures, are impossible to separate, and that, like the flow and the structure of time, these two grammars collide with each other all the time in our linguistic and textual practices: 'For Derrida, the separability of these two is precisely in question: can there be a pure thinking of a structure of time, unconstrained and uninflected by local, naturalising tendencies at work in worldly consciousness and restricted linguistic competences?' (2007, 40). The attempts of phenomenology to develop a pure realm of grammar, uncontaminated by the ordinary, uninflected by worldly notions of the past, present and future, is a delusion that Derrida systematically exposes. What is more, the collision of different conceptions of time, natural and unnatural, necessarily happens all the time, whether in the texts of phenomenology or, as I have been arguing, in the tendency of narrative to project the tensed into the untensed experience of time, confound the genetic and the static, or combine the flow and the structure of temporality.

When Derrida turns his attention to Marx, the unnatural is in the foreground, in the form of Hamlet's encounter with the ghost of his father on the ramparts of Elsinore, and time is out of joint. Both of these figures, the ghost and the disjuncture, are important for Derrida's elaboration of time in *Specters of Marx*, but the latter image is more closely related to his earlier stance on the problems of phenomenological distinctions. It might be more accurate to say that it is a figure of those problems, where the joint is the point of contact between one thing and another. The first chapter of *Specters of Marx* is, above all, a demonstration of the many ways that Hamlet's words might be brought to bear on the question of time, not least because the word time itself is so deeply equivocal:

> In 'The time is out of joint', time is either *le temps* itself, the temporality of time, or else what temporality makes possible (time as *histoire*, the way things are at a certain time, the time that we are living, nowadays, the period), or else, consequently, the *monde*, the world as it turns, our world today, currentness itself, current affairs . . . (2006, 20)

These are problems of translation, from French to English but also from one conception of time to another, and they are problems in particular for the idea that we might articulate the question of temporality as it is encountered in philosophy to the question of historical emergence or political action.

Playfully, it is the figure of disarticulation that most succeeds, in Derrida's discussion in articulating an account of temporality to an account of historical time. He begins with an account of what he calls the 'disjointure in the very presence of the present' which Heidegger finds in the fragment of Anaximander:

> To be sure, it says 'without equivocation' (eindeutig) that the present (das Anwesende), as present, is in *adikia*, that is, as Heidegger translates, deranged, off its hinges, out of joint (aus der Fuge). The present is what passes, the present comes to pass [se passe], it lingers in this transitory passage (Weile), in the coming-and-going, between what *goes* and what *comes*, in the middle of what leaves and what arrives, at the articulation between what absents itself and what presents itself. This in-between articulates conjointly the double articulation (die Fuge) according to which the two movements are adjoined (gefügt). Presence (Anwesen) is enjoined (verfügt), ordered, distributed in the two directions of absence, at the very articulation of what is no longer and what is not yet. (2006, 29–30)

This is an excellent statement, taken from the beginning of Western metaphysics, of the present as the articulation of what is no longer to what is not yet, the juncture between what leaves and what arrives, but it is difficult to ignore the fact that it has been translated from Greek to German, paraphrased by Heidegger, reparaphrased in French by Derrida, and translated into English. Worse than that, it is only one half of Derrida's paraphrase of Heidegger's paraphrase of the two halves of what is, according to Heidegger, said and not said by Anaximander. It is an excellent statement then, enfolded in an infuriating structure, which is, of course, meant to illustrate the 'radical untimeliness' that is involved when we try to 'think the ghost' (2006, 29). The other half of the statement, according to Heidegger, is concerned with justice, and the 'necessity of thinking justice on the basis of the gift'. There is here a translation of Anaximander into one of Heidegger and Derrida's favourite thematics on the subject of time: the notion that in gift theory there is a kind of aporetic logic which links the present as a gift to the temporal present. I will return shortly to this logic of the gift, which finds its way into so many of Derrida's later writings, but for the moment want only to observe its role in his introduction to the messianic, which is exactly a notion of the arrival of justice: 'the coming of the other, the absolute and unpredictable singularity of the *arrivant as justice*' (2006, 33).

Although this seems like a muddle of concepts, it is a muddle that derives from exactly the kind of collisions of different conceptions of time, of natural and unnatural languages, or the notion of flow and structure against which Husserl struggled. The notion of the messianic in Derrida is often glossed as the unpredictable future, but there are two dimensions that have to be added to the unpredictable before the concept properly comes into view. The first is a problem of the kind that we found in Grosz, of a certain tension between different temporal positions in relation to an event, one associated with explanation and understanding and the other with prospect, the first of which has the benefit of hindsight, of something having taken place, while the second anticipates but cannot know of a spontaneous emergence to come, of what will have happened. For Derrida, this tension is between teleology and eschatology, looking back on an event from an outcome, or looking forward to an outcome from an event, and we must discern between these two 'even if the stakes of such a difference risk constantly being effaced in the most fragile and slight insubstantiality – and will be in a certain way always and necessarily deprived of any insurance against this risk' (2006, 45). The messianic always carries within it this necessity and impossibility of separating teleology from eschatology, and each moment seems to carry within it a possible disruption from the unexpected:

Is there not a messianic extremity, an *eskhaton* whose ultimate event (immediate rupture, unheard-of-interruption, untimeliness of the infinite surprise,
heterogeneity without accomplishment) can exceed, *at each moment*, the final
term of a *phusis*, such as work, the production, and the *telos* of any history?
(2006, 45)

The logical relations in this question are undoubtedly muddled, and
trying to answer it is comically difficult. What does it mean to ask whether
something that cannot be foreseen *can exceed* the *telos* of any history? Is
it just that what is unforeseeable overshadows any envisaged outcome,
and that this is true at every moment of any history? If so, the *eskhaton*
of eschatology and the *telos* of teleology are indeed very difficult to separate. It is not the expectation or anticipation of an ending or outcome
that is at stake in this claim. It is the ultimate event of the *eskhaton*, not
the anticipation of it, which overshadows any idea of a predetermined
telos, but we cannot know that in advance. In a sense, the whole statement hinges on the word *can*, since it is the possibility, not the actuality,
of the ultimate event that gives structure to the present moment, but what
is the difference, then, between the possibility of an ultimate event and an
anticipation or expectation? Do we have to wait before we can determine
in retrospect whether the ultimate event did, in fact, exceed the *telos*. The
problems here are of temporal position. The difficulty of distinguishing
between a possibility and an unforeseeable event leads directly to the
difficulty of distinguishing eschatology from teleology, and both of these
result from a view of time always caught between flow and structure, or
the location in an inescapable present and the temporal perspective from
which structure comes into view without any such present moment. The
theoretical muddle, then, is Hodge's 'other time', which presents huge
difficulties for its expression because it escapes the ordinary view of time
as divided between past, present and future; and it is also the view in
which interruption, surprise, rupture and untimeliness are seen as more
basic than continuity or presence. The first thing we need to add to the
concept of unforeseeability for an understanding of messianic arrival,
then, is that if Husserl's account of time was stuck in 'the continuous
present of the living present', the messianic is the secret sharer in each
moment, according to which surprise is more basic.

The second dimension that needs to be added to the notion of ordinary unpredictability is the idea of the *arrivant as justice*. The phrase
seems to suggest that the messianic has a content, and therefore that we
can see what is to come in an event which is unforeseeable as a matter of
definition. In fact, this question of the content of messianicity brings
some clarity to the muddle of anticipation and ultimate event above. In
many of the most direct statements in *Specters of Marx*, Derrida is clear

that the concept of the messianic is exactly contentless: it is the 'strange concept of messianism without content, of the messianic without messianism' (2006, 82). Derrida's argument about Marxism entirely depends on this idea of contentlessness, in the sense that it allows him to abstract or empty out the content of messianism to leave only the temporal form of a promise, and without that content, the messianic works just as well as a description of the communist promise. The abstraction which empties the messianic of its messianism is also an important reorientation of the relationship between a future event and its anticipation in the present, of the kind that seemed to lie at the heart of the question of temporal position in the last paragraph. David Wood explains this in the following way: 'What Abrahamic religions understand as the future present, an event that could actually occur, Derrida understands as a structure of anticipation that cannot ever arrive or be completed' (Wood 2007, 52). In a sense, then, the whole question of tension between two views of time which cannot be reconciled, flow and structure, is reduced here to the view that the future can only ever exist in the present, and it exists as an impossible promise, or as an anticipation of an arrival that cannot come about. Derrida's favourite anecdote for the illustration of this impossible promise comes from Blanchot's joke about a man meeting the messiah at the gates of his city, and though the messiah has clearly arrived, the man asks him 'when will you come?'. Just as the arrival of the messiah has to be converted back into the structure of anticipation, so the promise in general cannot be fulfilled without losing its anticipatory structure. Wood comments as follows:

> What Derrida had once recognized as a structure of deferment (différance) is now being proposed as a permanent open anticipation of the possibility of a certain justice. The privilege of the future that Heidegger had promoted in *Being and Time* is not being drawn into a broader ecstatic dimensionality as it is in *On Time and Being*. Rather, the very significance of time is being recast in economic and ethical terms. The to-come (a-venir) makes the future into a hope and a promise built into the present. Symmetrically, the true 'event' is not grasped in advance. (2007, 52–3)

The event can only arise in the absence of anticipation. It must arrive without appearing in any horizon of expectation, from above, and this means that the promise must be without specific content; it must be the permanent open anticipation of a hope without content. What, then, is justice if not the content of the anticipated arrival? The answer can only be that it is not specific content, but rather the qualitative nature of the future orientation, which Derrida refers to variously as one of optimism, hospitality and openness, as openness to the singularity of the arrival, and, following Levinas, as an unconditional hospitality to the stranger, or to the other. The optimistic quality of the anticipation, combined with its contentlessness, is where politics and ethics reside.

Bearing in mind Derrida's insistence that this impossible arrival is impossible to think about, and that it presents grave problems of expression within the ordinary conception of time and the tense structure of natural language, we do nevertheless have a basic list of properties on which to assess the political and ethical responsibility of the messianic. The messianic is the anticipation of the unforeseeable, a recognition that time must be thought through aporia, a strategic commitment to the view that interruption is more basic than continuous presence, a view that anticipation can never be completed, that the arrival is impossible, and so that the anticipation cannot have content, and finally, a view that the anticipation without content can nevertheless ascribe the quality of justice to the event that it cannot foresee. Even with the invocation of Levinas that runs through this argument, it is difficult to see more here, in terms of the value of the unexpected as an ethical or political concept, than Grosz's ultimate sense of the natural opacity of the future. Interestingly, those moments in Derrida's corpus that engage most fully with Levinas's work tend not to reach for the concept of the messianic but to display a preference for the tense structure of the future anterior. This is most strikingly the case in the essay 'At This Very Moment in This Work Here I Am', first published in French in 1980 and becoming widely available in translation only with the publication of *Psyche: Inventions of the Other Volume 1* in 2007. The dates are important here because they mix up, for an English readership, the discussion of the messianic with the earlier interest in the future anterior. Just as it is possible to see the messianic in terms of a direct continuity from the early analyses of Husserl's distinctions, so too we find, in Derrida's discussion of Levinas in this essay, a clear basis for linking the messianic with the future anterior. Derrida begins the essay with a future anterior structure that organises the whole discussion, 'He will have obligated [Il aura obligé]'; these words are themselves repeated, cited again and again, and so too the tense is used repeatedly in other sentences. One of the more tantalising declarations that Derrida makes about the significance of the tense is that 'the future anterior could be – and this resemblance is irreducible – the time of Hegelian teleology,' and we should understand by this something like Ricoeur's definition of teleological explanation in general. But as soon as he has said so, he also says the opposite, that the future anterior designates exactly the thing that cannot be reduced to Hegelian or philosophical teleology, and here we see another instance of the argument about the inseparability of teleology and eschatology:

From the moment it is in accord with the 'he' as Pro-noun of the wholly other 'always already past', it will have drawn toward an eschatology without philosophical teleology, beyond it in any case, otherwise than it. It will have thrust the future anterior toward the bottomless depth of a past anterior to any past, toward that passing or passed [passée] of the trace that has never been present. Its future anteriority will have been irreducible to ontology. To an ontology, moreover, designed to attempt this impossible reduction. (2007, 176)

Something happens as soon as the words of this sentence connect up that makes the apparent time of the future anterior, as an anticipation of something that is complete, move in a different direction. The future anterior, according to this, is no more teleological than it is eschatological, and here again we see the difficulty of distinguishing between the idea of waiting for an outcome from which to look back and explain the present, and speculating impossibly on an outcome that lies ahead and which, like the arrival of the messiah, cannot arrive. In this crossover, what is more, the idea of presence and the idea of ontology are both casualties. As soon as these words *he will have obligated* combine, some event in the future is set off that is always already past: the words *will have* drawn toward eschatology, they *will have* thrust the future anterior into a condition of non-presence, and the future anterior *will have* been irreducible to ontology. The future anterior, in other words, is both the subject of these claims and the tense of their verbs.

It is easy to lose patience with Derrida in these sections as he begins to perform the temporality in question, but there is a pay-off for the understanding of narrative in this particular entanglement of the messianic and the future anterior. The ordinary understanding of the words *he will have obligated* would be to take them to refer to an unidentified person who, at some time in the future, succeeded in bringing about an obligation. To verify this we would have to be located after the action referred to, after the obligation has been brought about. Neither the 'he' of the utterance nor the 'we' of this verification are therefore present when the action came about, since it happens in 'his' future and in 'our' past. For him, the action is deferred, and for us, it is complete. Between us we satisfy both sides of the future anterior's contract, the necessary deferral of futurity and the completion of the grammatical *perfectus*, or, in Derrida's language, the deferral of eschatology and the completion of teleology. Supposing, for the sake of illustration, we were to give some more detail to this cryptic fragment and make a new sentence: *John will have obligated me by giving me a present.* We might then say that, for John, this action of obligating me is never present (the present is never present) because it is in the future tense, but because it is in the future perfect tense it carries its completion with it in advance. This means that it is not only in the contract between John and me that we satisfy both sides of the contract, but that, for John on his own, the action is always both futural and complete. Two quite different things are colliding here, one of which is the co-presence of futurity and completion in the moment of utterance, while the other is a question of verification, which requires a position of retrospect in order to assign truth to the utterance. For John, the future anterior of his act of giving will always have to wait upon confirmation, and for me, hindsight alone will allow the assessment of the original utterance in terms of truth. These are the two things that, according to Derrida, will always collide: the future-orientation of the moment and the position of verification of that moment later. It may be easy to lose patience with Derrida as he begins to perform the temporality in question, but it is exactly this combination of the moment of time flow and the structure of retrospect that requires this performance, in which the future anterior is both the predicate of the verb and the object of study:

> That future anteriority *there* would no longer conjugate a verb describing the action of a subject in an operation that would have been *present*. To say 'he will have obligated' – in *this* work, taking into account what makes the work within this seriasure – is not to designate, describe, define, show and so on, but let us say, to entrace, in other words to perform within the intr(el)acement of a seriasure this obligation of which 'he' will not have been the present subject but for which 'I' hereby answer. Here I am, (I) come. (2007, 176; original italics)

We can see here some of Derrida's earlier preoccupations mutating towards the messianic. Future anteriority more or less shows itself to be the same structure as the messianic without messianism: that is to say, an empty or contentless temporal structure that can nevertheless be characterised as an obligation. The difference between the conjugation of a verb and the acts of designating, describing, defining and showing takes the tension between the tense of the verb and the verification of truth in the direction of another distinction between performative and constative utterances; the future anterior does not so much describe as perform the obligation in question. The obligation is present neither to 'he' nor to 'I'; it is an anticipation for Levinas (the *el* in intrelacement) which is met by an arrival, an 'I' who comes to answer. To complete the list of properties of the messianic, we can even find, in this coming of the 'I' who hereby answers, the theme of interruption, a word that Emmanuel Levinas 'uses often', which is repeated as often, in Derrida's discussion, as the future anterior itself. We have, in other words, in the future anterior, a tense structure for the arrival of the unexpected, an impossible arrival which promotes interruption above presence, which anticipates without having any content, and which yet has the characteristics of a moral or political responsibility. In the essay on Levinas, in other words, we have a comprehensive basis on which to regard the future anterior and the messianic, the strange combination, on one hand, of anticipation and retrospect, and the unforeseeable arrival, on the other, as the same structure.

The synthesis of the future anterior and the messianic might play its part in an obscure corner of philosophy, in the deconstruction of time, but its basic tension is writ large in narrative. Whether we think of this structure as a reference to future time with built-in completion, or as an anticipation of something that cannot arrive, we have a description of the essential contentlessness of anticipation, the empty *something* in the phrases *something will happen* and *something will have happened*. This is not to say that we cannot anticipate something concrete, whether in dread or hope, but rather that any specific content cannot be displaced, confirmed or negated by the arrival of the future and preserve its character as anticipation. Something quite simple and quite complex comes into view in the synthesis, simple because it reaffirms the platitude that tomorrow never comes, and complex because it reminds us that we must always reach for a different conception of time, according to which the anticipation itself must refer to an event that is already past, in order to make sense of the ordinary conception of time as a series of present moments. It is doubtful, for this reason, that we can invoke the notion of the unexpected on behalf of any specifically political temporal predicament, and yet also evident that it would be impossible to think about change unless standing on this junction, the place of collision, of the still to come and the already complete.

PART III
Time Flow and the Process of Reading

Chapter 6

Narrative Modality: Possibility, Probability and the Passage of Time

In the previous two chapters we have encountered, in Mallarmé and Badiou, but also in Nietzsche and Grosz, a thematisation of action as a kind of wager or bet upon what will have happened. The idea of the future as a wager suggests probability as a more obvious mathematics of the future perfect than set theory. There can be no question that our cognitive control of the future must involve us in an assessment of the probability of events that we foresee, and it seems likely that the events that we do not foresee are the lowest probability events. The unexpected event is essentially an improbable event, one which stands out from everyday routine, established reality or the inductive reasoning of common expectation, and is essentially unpredictable in the manner of the black swan. The prediction of a high probability event, we remarked in Chapter 4, is worth little when compared with the prediction of an improbable one, which means that we are seeking refuge from tautology in contradiction, since it suggests that the prediction of the predictable is worthless, whereas predicting the unpredictable is worthwhile. This is the predicament, of course, if we think only in terms of opposition, in terms of the maximal difference between the predictable and the unpredictable, and it is for the deflation of that hyperbole that we value probability.

The grammatical category that most closely reflects the value we place on probability is modality. If tense is the most obvious marker of temporality in language, capable of encoding the most complex relationships between the time of an utterance and the time of events to which it refers, the degree of certainty of a proposition or of the potential occurrence of an event, its probability or possibility, is carried by modality. Both tense and modality have a certain kind of explanatory power in relation to narrative, especially in its tilt towards the future, but whereas the category of tense has at least been a constant source of descriptive resource for the narratologist, modality has much looser foothold in the

narratological universe, despite the fact that it is the place where probability and possibility are assessed and communicated in language.
There are some obvious reasons for this. Modality can be said to have
two functions, one of which is to express the degree of certainty, possibility and probability of events (epistemic modality), while the other is
to lay down instructions, obligations or permissions (deontic modality),
and it can be argued that narrative is not primarily or obviously involved
in either of these linguistic functions. So, for example, a standard narrative sentence – 'It was a dark and stormy night' – commits itself to the
factuality of its proposition, and therefore differs in the degree of certainty expressed from sentences which do not seem to deal in facts in the
same way: 'It might have been a dark and stormy night'; 'It must have
been a dark and stormy night'. These latter sentences can be thought of
as modifying the degree of certainty expressed by the former proposition, and therefore differ in the degree of subjectivity they express,
between a speaker who knows that what they say is true and one who is
not quite sure. Sentences can be placed on a spectrum between certainty
and doubt according to the exigencies of possibility, probability and
necessity in the case of epistemic modality, or of volition, obligation and
permission in the case of deontic modality.

In *Story Logic*, David Herman assembles some of the attitudes that
have excluded modality from consideration in classical narratology. He
cites Genette's remark:

> Since the function of narrative is not to give an order, express a wish, state a
> condition, etc., but simply to tell a story and therefore to 'report' facts (real
> or fictive), its one mood, or at least its characteristic mood, strictly speaking,
> can be only the indicative. (Genette 1980, 161)

Gerald Prince offers a similar view that the basic modality of narrative
is the expression of certainty rather than doubt: 'Narrative, which is ety-
mologically linked to knowledge, lives in certainty (this happened then
that; this happened because of that; this happened and it was related to
that) and dies from (sustained) ignorance or indecision' (Prince 1982,
4). Narrative, in other words, deals in certainty because it relates what
has taken place, and the assessment of possibility and probability, as
encoded in epistemic modality, is not generally a feature of narrative
sentences. Against these views of narrative's basic mood, Herman
objects that 'all narratives encode different degrees of certainty with
respect to what is narrated':

> Exploiting the same epistemic modalities operative in a discourse at large,
> narrative discourse characteristically indicates how much credence readers

should place in any one proposition found in the text. Debatably, extended narrative discourse has evolved into the pre-eminent resource for perspective taking precisely because it accomplishes such a wide range of epistemic stances, chaining together in a single discourse propositions more or less widely spaced along the scale by which degrees of certainty are encoded in discourse. (Herman 2002, 327–8)

It is particularly in focalisation that narrative can stage these perspectives of greater or lesser certainty, greater or lesser degrees of objectivity, so that a sentence like 'It must have been a dark and stormy night' is perfectly imaginable as emanating from a located subjectivity, whether that of a narrator or character, who had not been outdoors. But Herman wants to go beyond this kind of traditional focalisation, in which uncertainty is the mark of the focalised subjectivity, to account for narrative's ability to imagine perspectives other than the ones dramatised by characters or narrators, in order to show that the kind of analytical resources neglected by traditional narratology, such as those of epistemic modality, can, in fact, be put to use by narratologists. Epistemic modality is particularly useful, then, for what Herman calls 'hypothetical focalization', which 'entails the use of hypotheses, framed by the narrator or a character, about what might be, or might have been seen or perceived – if only there were someone who could have adopted the requisite perspective on the situations and events at issue' (2002, 303). Hypothetical focalisation, then, involves the concoction of some non-existent focaliser, or some non-existent perspective as an alternative to those dramatised in a fictional narrative, as when A. S. Byatt's narrator in *Possession* concocts a witness to speculate on the main characters from the outside: 'An observer might have speculated for some time as to whether they were travelling together or separately' (1991, 297). At the level of grammatical form, such a hypothesis is an example of how a narrative might make use of modal expressions (not 'she speculated' but 'she might have speculated') despite its default modality of the declarative or indicative statement. It is also borrowing from another set of ideas, which have developed the idea of modality beyond the level of grammatical form, in possible worlds philosophy and possible worlds semantics, which have concerned themselves with the representation of non-actual states that might be thought to exist in parallel with the actual state of affairs. Possibility and hypotheticality, from this point of view, are not temporal or futural; the possible is a non-actual perspective which could have taken place, which might have happened, if there had been someone there to adopt it, as an alternative perspective to the actual focalisation of the narrative. Around the category of focalisation, then, Herman formulates the following project:

I do not mean to suggest that the present analysis has thrown new light on all of the narrative phenomena discussed in earlier research on focalization. My purpose has been only to give some initial indications of how narrative theorists might embark on such a redescription. In this connection, [hypothetical focalization] is, I believe, an especially diagnostic problem domain; it shows that, in order to come to terms with the cognitive dimensions of narrative perspective, researchers need to bridge narratological accounts of focalization and ideas drawn from semantic theory. (2002, 328)

What interests me in this call for the redescription of focalisation is that a particular semantic theory underlies the formula of how epistemic modality can be linked to narrative, and it is one that has functioned to sever a fundamental link between modality and futurity. The category of focalisation is particularly interesting here, if only because the notion of hypothetical focalisation is not the most direct way of linking modality with narrative theory, given that focalisation is also the key mechanism by which a narrative locates a reader in narrative time, and controls the distribution of knowledge across time, in relation to which the events of a narrative sequence are already or not yet known. Focalisation certainly does have an important relationship with epistemic modality, but the account of modality that narratology has derived from possible worlds theory restricts its ability to describe this strong relation. Another way of saying the same thing is to look more carefully at the language of Herman's definition of hypothetical focalisation: 'what might be, or might have been seen'. The alternative modal expressions here point us towards a more general difficulty of separating the modality of alternative possibility from the modality of future time reference; a trace of the future, of the modalised future and the modalised future perfect, inhabits both of these expressions. What they seem to present is an interesting invitation, on top of the basic call for a redescription of focalisation, to extend the description of narrative modality in such a way that it encompasses, as well as the modality of alternative possibility, the semantics of future time reference. When focalisation is thought of in terms of the temporal location of characters or narrators (their location in a moment), there may also be a temporal species of focalisation, understood as a hypothetical perspective on what might have been seen if only there were someone there who knew the future, or occupied a position of retrospect (a location in a future moment, an omniscience across time) from which that moment is understood, and it will be one of the aims of this argument to show that narrative is centrally concerned with this kind of hypothesis. This notion of hypotheticality, as retrospect which does not exist in the moment, as the projection of the future perfect, the hypothesis of what might have happened, is clearly present in Herman's next paragraph, when narrative is considered in one of its more decisively future-orientated settings, as coaching:

> In their study of the instructional register of coaching, Shirley Brice Heath and Juliet Langman (1994) found that 'eventcasts', or hypothetical descriptions of what might happen in game situations, are an important instrument for building the knowledge repertoire of team members. (2002, 328)

For Herman, this shows that 'hypotheticality in discourse need not always have the function of conveying uncertainty or doubt,' but it does also connect one issue in narrative modality with the other: just as narrative has the power to stage the co-existence of doubt and certainty, it also has a special power to join the uncertainty of prospect to the certainty of retrospect. Eventcasts are indeed interesting indications of the importance of narrative as a means of imagining the future, and the ubiquity of stories as preparation for the unexpected, in contexts as diverse as financial planning, political scenario modelling and health and safety training demonstrates this. But there is also a sense in which this is a cognitive function of narrative more generally, beyond the category of the eventcast, and that we can think of narrative focalisation in particular exactly as a mechanism for the cognitive grasp of the future. The temporalisation of narrative focalisation – that is to say, the analysis of temporal dimensions of perspectival and information distributions in narrative – might help us to come to terms with these cognitive dimensions of narrative discourse. A redescription of focalisation of this kind might then turn to semantic theories concerned with the modality of those most uncertain of propositions – future time statements. The interest in the modality of future time statements is increased considerably by the presence of arguments in semantics that modality is not just a system of linguistic markers encoding possibility and probability, but that modality is identical with time itself.

In being concerned with certainty, the notion of epistemic modality is also deeply concerned with time. A straightforward, or unmodalised statement (*there is a monster upstairs*) commits itself to fact, or demonstrates a high level of certainty. The modalisation of this statement, by adding words such as *will, must, should, ought, may, might* or *could*, diminishes the certainty of this proposition (*there must be a monster upstairs, there may be a monster upstairs*), even if, as in the case of *must*, the modalisation seems to carry the meaning of necessity – *there must be a monster upstairs* expresses less certainty than *there is a monster upstairs*. A connection is apparent from the start between the category of epistemic modality and the temporal reference of the statement concerned, since *there is a monster upstairs* refers to the present, whereas *there may be a monster upstairs* expresses a hint of future time reference, or some degree of detachment from the state of affairs described. In her study of temporality and modality, Kasia Jaszczolt relies heavily on this notion of detachment in order to claim that the certainty encoded in modalisation is difficult to separate from temporal detachment:

> Within the category of epistemic modality, just as modal expressions *may*, *can*, *might* or *could* express a certain detachment from the state of affairs expressed in the proposition, so the indicators of temporality in the form of past and future markers express a certain detachment from the certainty of *now*. And, just as modal expressions *must* or *have to* express a high degree of probability or even certainty on behalf of the speaker, so the indicators of present time express a high degree of probability that the state of affairs is in reality just as described in the speaker's sentence. (2009, 38)

There is, in other words, a certain conspiracy between certainty and presence, bordering on circularity, whereby modal expressions and temporal indicators co-operate to express degrees of a speaker's detachment from the content of a proposition. There is also a metaphysical question – a certain metaphysics of presence – that shows itself here in the reciprocity between the concept of certainty and the concept of presence, but if this is so it is a question with which Jaszczolt does not concern herself, on the grounds that her project is to 'build semantic representations of temporality and to demonstrate that for doing this modal concepts will suffice' (2009, 39). The relationship between epistemic modality and the concept of time is one of logical dependency, or what she calls 'supervenience', which is to say that time is not a primitive concept, in the sense that it existed first and on its own, but one which needs the linguistic expression of possibility and probability before it can come into existence. This is not to say that the universe would stop expanding if there were no modal expressions in human language, but that the concept of time and the human (i.e. internal, psychological) experience of time require modality for their form and content.

The reality that Jaszczolt is concerned with is the cognitive reality of time, so that the enquiry in semantics begins from the assumption that 'the semantic representation of temporal expressions requires a perspective that reflects the cognitive reality of human conceptualizations of time and at the same time offers a formal account of meaning' (2009, 96). The semantic representation of temporality, therefore, and unsurprisingly, reflects the cognitive reality of time, which is internal time, and in this relationship the notion of epistemic detachment has a special descriptive power, since internal time can be thought of as internal detachment from certainty. One of the properties of internal time that Jaszczolt sets against what she calls real time is the so-called flow of time, and the notion of modality allows this flow to be described in terms of certainty:

> not only is it the case that real time does not flow while internal time does but also the internal time itself, i.e. *the time that flows*, is conceptualized as flowing from the probabilities of the future into the certainty of *now* and out of the certainty of *now* into the fragmented picture, and hence uncertainty of the past. (2009, 50)

This description does not quite do justice to the asymmetry of time as most philosophers have seen it, whereby time flows from possibility into actuality but not back again – from the open future into a fixed rather than an uncertain past – nor is it consonant with the view cited earlier that the indicative mode of narrative retrospect is essentially one of certainty. There is, I would say, some crossover here between the view that the present has some special ontological status (that things exist in the present, but not in the future or the past) and a view that the present has some special epistemological status (that things are certain in the present, but uncertain in the future or the past), and that the asymmetry of time requires that references to the past be graded as more certain than references to the future. Jaszczolt does, in fact, direct some energy in her argument towards establishing that the past should be thought of as uncertain when compared with now and that it should be thought, along with the future, in terms of possibility, but there is also a recognition throughout that in discourse the future is marked by modal expressions to an extent that the past is not, and that the relationship of the future to modal expressions is much more clearly established in semantic theory than it is for the past. I dwell on this because it will be important for my argument about epistemic modality in narrative that retrospect carries a greater degree of certainty than prospect, and that this is the basis on which narrative welds possibility to actuality in a sequence. What is important, in any case, is that, in terms of gradations of certainty, the future is least certain, to the point that it can be difficult to disentangle the future tense as such from epistemic modality. This is a problem that arises particularly in relation to languages such as English where there is no future tense morpheme, and future time reference is constructed in a broad range of expressions, many of which are inflected with degrees of uncertainty. In addition to some of the foundational arguments that link the future to modality in general (Fleischman 1982), there are many arguments that also show that the future tense is interwoven with an intention to convey degrees of probability (Wekker 1976) or that 'will' in English is ambiguous between being a future tense marker and a modal expression with a force similar to that of *must* (Hornstein 1990). To make things worse, there are clearly forms of future time reference which cannot really be thought of as future tenses at all, such as what Fleischman calls the go-future (*I am going to make a cup of coffee*), which Declerck (2006) calls a 'futurish' tense form because it is a present progressive with a dual time reference: the present moment of the prediction and the future moment that it predicts. The difficulty of linking tense to temporal reference can be said to exist for any tense, and it is easy to demonstrate that almost any time can be referred to in almost any tense (see Crystal 2002), but the problem is exacerbated in the case of future time reference because of the degree of detachment, in terms of time and certainty, that necessarily accompanies any excursion into the inaccessible, and therefore uncertain (however probable) future. In Jaszczolt's argument, the difficulty of establishing tense as the basis of temporal reference, along with the intertwining of modal and temporal detachment, suggests that modality, the evaluation of the likelihood of a situation, is a more basic category than tense, more basic, in fact, than the flow of time, from which the notion of temporality can be derived: 'we can conclude that the concept of the future is detachment, prediction, graded commitment . . . without any clear reliance on the concept of time flow,' which is to say that if modality is the underlying concept in the concept of time, that time flow is 'composed out of the underlying modal time and the emergent property of movement' (2009, 62). There are two strands in this argument about modality that I want to pursue in relation to narrative. The first is that modality might be regarded not only as a complement to the category of tense, but as a concept more basic to the temporality of discourse than tense; the second is that modality might be more basic to an understanding of time itself than the notion of temporal flow. Before doing so, it will be necessary to assess the extent of influence of the notion of epistemic modality in the current conception of narrative.

The temporality of possible worlds

The word *possible* has two possible meanings, one of which is concerned with contingency and the other concerned with futurity. As contingency, possibility is the notion that an actual situation could be otherwise, or that there are other, non-actual states of affairs which exist in parallel with the state of affairs that exists. As futurity, possibility is the existence of a situation in the future which may nor may not pass into the actuality of the present. Like the cross-contamination of the future tense with modal expressions in general, these two possibilities are difficult to disentangle from a semantic point of view, since the notion of a contingent possibility carries within it a supposition that it could have happened (the modal future perfect) but did not. One of the places in which these two kinds of modality, the probability of other possible situations and the probability of future events, have figured in narrative theory is in the use that narratologists have made of possible worlds theory and possible worlds semantics for an understanding of narrative modality. It is my proposition, however, that the temporality of possible worlds, which is to say the futurity of possibility, has been the neglected pole of this dyad, and that, surprisingly perhaps, narrative theory has generally avoided the question of what we do not yet know in a narrative to focus instead on the more spatial, perspectival contingency of point of view. We have seen this already in Herman's discussion of epistemic modality in relation to focalisation, where hypothetical focalisation is the invocation of 'what might be, or might have been seen' alongside the perspective in which we are saddled, but it is also Herman's injunction to redescribe focalisation with the use of resources that were not available to classical narratology that we will be following here: to redescribe focalisation in its temporal dimension, as the distribution of certainty over time.

The notion of possible worlds, as it has been adapted from Leibniz for modal logic, is, to a large degree, the explanation for the non-temporal notion of possibility that has governed narratological approaches to modality. There is, as Ruth Ronen has shown with great clarity, a considerable diversity of philosophical positions encompassed under the heading of possible worlds theory, but the kernel is invariably non-temporal, or what the structuralists called *paradigmatic*, in the sense that the theory involves an attempt to think about the existence of non-actual states which might be thought to exist in parallel with the actual state of affairs. If one understanding of these alternative possibilities is that they are states of affairs that could have happened, efforts to theorise fiction as a possible world have generally abandoned that emphasis on plausibility, or what Aristotle called probability, in order to accommodate fiction that represents impossible things. To accommodate such fictions, we have to think of possible worlds as imaginative projections of the non-actual rather than as future possibilities of things that might come about, or might have come about. But in thinking like this, literary theoretical versions of possible worlds have already taken sides in a philosophical debate by detaching the notion of the possible world from the relative probability of its occurrence: they have sided with a view of possible worlds as parallel ontological worlds in which no special status is accorded to the actual world in terms of the semantic operations by which this world is constructed, so that possibility and probability can mean much more than the fidelity of a representation to the actual world. Ronen argues that this position is favoured by literary theorists because it allows for a certain dissolution of the distinction between actual and non-actual worlds, and therefore enables the transferability of possible worlds semantics to the imaginative worlds of literature. Ronen also argues that the weakening of this distinction is a way for literary theory to re-establish fiction as an object of philosophical attention, as opposed to a discourse without truth value, and even as a way in which issues of reference can be readmitted to literary studies after what Pavel calls the 'moratorium on referential issues' (1986, 10) associated with structuralism. Though these questions, which relate mainly to the question of fiction and reality, are interesting as an account of what literary criticism and theory have to gain from an engagement with possible worlds semantics, they are not the questions that most concern me here. They do, however, offer an account of the way that possible worlds tends to be used as a way of establishing ontological equivalence between possible worlds, and therefore of detaching the notion from its foundation, in modal logic, of the relative probability or possibility of events. I want to leave this question of the logical status of fictional discourse aside for a moment until we have asked the question of how narratology has developed the basic propositions of possible worlds into analytical methods for narrative semantics. Like Herman, Ronen's account of possible worlds in narrative analysis turns to the category of focalisation on the grounds that it is the perspectival structure of a narrative that generates its modally structured universe, and particularly the relative authority of the assembled perspectives:

> A perspectival arrangement of elements generates a modally structured universe. Yet in fiction, as has been noticed by several scholars ... the authority of fictional speakers and narrators determines the factual or non-factual nature of propositions about the fictional universe; that is, as readers of fiction we follow the authoritative say-so of a speaker in establishing the facts of fiction ... Once a speaker has been situated outside the fictional world with omniscience and omnipotence on his side, the events and situations narrated are likely to be viewed by the reader as facts of the fictional world. (Ronen 1994, 176)

If, in the first place, the notion of modality is directed towards the modal status of fictional worlds, the narratological project that it licenses seems to be no more than a perception that the fictional universe is normally constituted by voices of differing degrees of certainty, authority, objectivity and externality. This is not to say that the authority of facts in fiction is underwritten by any appeal to the actuality of facts in the outside world; rather the basis for authority is internal and hierarchical, where 'facts, quasi-facts and non-facts constitute the totality of the world' and where fictional facts exist alongside 'sets of relativized elements attributed to characters' knowledge, beliefs, thoughts and predictions' (1994, 176). Like Herman, Ronen takes the fictional world as one that is 'fundamentally modal' in the sense that it is comprised of statements of differing degrees of certainty according to the externality of their perspective.

It is interesting to chart the ways in which this conception of narrative as a modally structured world detaches itself from temporality, not only in Ronen's analysis but also in the more general tendency to translate futural possibility into contingent possibility that characterises possible worlds narratology. Ryan (1991) begins her discussion of the modal structure of narrative universes by pointing out that French structuralist narratologists had stressed the importance of non-factual events in the early 1970s:

> Bremond distinguishes two types of narrative statements: descriptive statements, which recount actual events; and modalized statements, which 'anticipate the hypothesis of a future event, of a virtual action' . . . Todorov distinguishes four modal operators for narrative propositions: the *obligatory* mode, for events dictated by the laws of society; the *optative* mode, for states and actions desired by the characters; the *conditional* mode, expressing action to which characters commit themselves if certain other events happen; and the *predictive* mode, for anticipated events. (Ryan 1991, 110)

In Bremond's case, it is clear that modalised statements are entirely concerned with futurity, and that virtual action is action that lies ahead as future possibility. In Todorov's case, the four modal operators are futural to different degrees, with the predictive mode being the most directly linked to anticipation of the future. But Ryan is swift in her translation:

> These observations are easily restated in the terminology of the present model. Bremond's descriptive statements are the states and events of the actual world of the narrative universe while his modalized statements describe the alternative possible worlds of the system. Todorov's catalog of modalities is an embryonic typology of [alternative possible worlds]. (1991, 110)

In other contexts, structuralist narratologists are routinely accused of a spatialisation of narrative time and, in particular, a tendency to translate temporal process into oppositions, or the spatial relations of selection and combination. In this one, the category of temporal possibility is simply displaced by the notion of possibility as alternative possible world, and modality's link to anticipation and prediction is severed. Ronen works her way through this process more patiently in a chapter that describes the dead end of structuralist plot-models for narrative. Classical (structuralist) narratology is, for Ronen, obsessed with the isolation of narrative units which promote a syntactic and anti-referential view of narrative, as well as being riddled with fallacies about the importance of causality as a principle of narrative organisation. Narrative semantics, on the other hand, offers narratology a response to the anti-referential ideology of structuralism – a response that Ronen regards as capable of overcoming the 'theoretical discrepancy, so typical of structuralist poetics, between paradigmatic rules and syntactic operations' (1994, 172). In theory, then, possible worlds semantics is not a translation of temporal modality into contingent modality, but rather a way of combining the paradigmatic rules of narrative logic with operational rules for describing plot movement. In practice, however, the final two chapters of Ronen's discussion are clear cases of the tendency to subordinate the question of temporal possibility to the concept of logical contingency. The first of these turns, as we have seen, to the question of focalisation, or, more specifically, to the interaction between entities and focalisers which 'produces a world structured according to varying degrees of authenticity', but focalisation here is primarily understood in spatial terms. This is partly a result of a decision made by Ronen in the pursuit of her argument to 'concentrate on one fictional domain composed of a set of spatial entities, or of places' (1994, 180). The point about this decision is that it chooses to focus on perspectival arrangements in relation to places and therefore to focus on the spatial located-ness of internal perspectives as compared with the relative lack of perspectival restraints that characterises external focalisation. We should therefore assume that, had the decision been otherwise, the analysis might have been otherwise, and might have concentrated instead on temporal location: that place is just one contingent dimension of focalisation among others. But there is some reason to think that the whole notion of narrative focus contains an anti-temporal presupposition: that it is a visual metaphor which carries an ineluctable connotation of place and space. Ronen, for example, cites Hamburger's definition of narrative focus as the 'here and now' of fiction, a concept in itself fairly balanced between time and space, but which is explicitly linked by Hamburger to present time – 'even if a "present time" . . . is not indicated at all . . . we experience the action of the novel as being "here and now" as the experience of fictive persons' – but her commentary reasserts the priority of place – 'A *narrative focus*, like a perceptual position, functions as a type of focalization motivating modes of arranging places (or other fictional entities)' (1994, 186). But, as Jaszczolt points out (2009, 70), the notion of a focus or focal point is just as easily connected in semantic theory as it is in Prior's tense logic, with the notion of *now* as it is to the notion of *here*. In order to give this apparent preference the benefit of the doubt, we then have to turn to Ronen's final chapter, which deals with fictional time, but even here we find a preference for the paradigmatic and the spatial of the kind that possible worlds theory invariably imports into narrative theory. Ronen's discussion is, in fact, one of the best things written on the subject of fictional time, but it takes its place in a book concerned primarily with the idea of fiction as a parallel world. In this spirit, the analysis is concerned with the question of fiction as an analogy for the spatiotemporal conditions that pertain in the actual world, and takes the position from the outset that fiction constructs a parallel and autonomous temporal system which relates to real time in the manner of a metaphorical substitution: it is similar, but different. Because there is no objective sequence of events which underlies events as told in a fiction, the notion of chronology is understood, with Barbara Hernstein Smith, as a metaphor, in the sense that it is merely analogous to the notion of chronology that pertains in real time. The same thing is argued in relation to the narrative present, a foundational notion for most accounts of the temporality of narrative:

> In view of the complex relations between narrative present and basic notions of time, my counter-proposal to this first notion of temporality in fiction is grounded in the nature of the narrative present. My claim is that definitions of the narrative present reflect the temporality associated with fiction. The present, which is literally a temporal concept, works as a metaphorical substitute for a modal concept . . . (1994, 210)

The concepts of narrative present and fictional present are, Ronen argues, like any other aspect of fictional time, perspectivally determined, and are better thought of as modal concepts. The present is not really the present at all in a narrative but, Ronen argues, a narrative level that we think of as present because it differs from other levels in its degree of immediacy and actuality. The fictional present in particular is not comparable with the present of real time because it does not progress through time in any way that is separate from its perspectival context: 'the delimitation of the fictive present follows the specific modal structure of a given fictional universe; each narrative text selects different (and not necessarily temporal) materials to be actualized as its present' (1994, 211).

There are two strands in this kind of argument, the first of which is concerned with the relation between narrative temporality and real time, and which aims to show that any discrepancy between the two is an indication that narrative time is non-actual; the second is a tendency to reduce temporality to modal structures concerned not only with questions of temporal location and organisation but also with degrees of perspectival immediacy and actuality. In both strands, modality carries the meaning of hypotheticality over and above the meaning of futurity, and there is an encumbent tendency to erase futural meanings of modality as part of the reduction, sometimes denial, of narrative temporality. As the earlier discussion of focalisation preferred the *here* to the *now* in its discussion of narrative focus, so the discussion of time systematically subordinates or erases temporal dimensions of modality, or characterises temporal terminology as metaphors for modal concepts, as if modal concepts were not implicated in temporal location. When Ronen is in pursuit of the argument that the narrative present is a metaphor for a modal concept, for example, she cites Helen Dry's article 'The Movement of Narrative Time': 'situations on a time line . . . are presented as actually occurring in the narrative world, as opposed to being merely talked of, expected, or hypothesized' (Dry 1983, 21). The contrast between 'actually occurring' and 'talked of, expected or hypothesized' – which, in the case of 'expected', is unambiguously a relation between present and future – does not survive in Ronen's commentary, which remarks that the criterion of presentness is 'internal' and 'unrelated to extranarrative temporality', so that the temporal relationship is speedily recast in terms of paradigmatic possibility or the modality of parallel worlds, through the idea of the discrepancy between fictional and real time. Her conclusions about the two key properties of fictional time repeat the gesture:

> The first property of fictional time that emerges from its particular mode of being is connected to the fact that time in fiction constitutes a parallel and autonomous temporal system; the second property is related to the correlation between temporal relations and the degree of actuality of a given fictional situation (whether a situation is an actual state of affairs in the story, or only a hypothetical or talked about state of affairs). (1994, 227)

Here the point about the autonomy of fictional time in relation to actual time is attached to an observation about a different kind of actuality – the degrees of actuality that differentiate the 'actually occurring' from the hypothetical. But if this conclusion echoes the language of Dry's list of non-actual occurrences – the trinity of 'talked of, expected, or hypothesized' – it is important that the most futural word is omitted from the conclusion.

What I am suggesting here is that a different account of focalisation, and therefore of the *moving now* of narrative and fiction, is required for the description of narrative temporality. It seems necessary, in particular, that the question of *now* is restored to an account of the distribution of knowledge, actuality and certainty that structures a narrative, and so to understand the perspectival structures of focalisation in terms of temporal position: of what is certain, what is expected and what is unexpected. A different account of *now*, of the narrative present, is not one that seeks to conflate the semiotic notion of now with that of lived experience, or to deny that a discrepancy exists between fictional and real time, but one that aims to describe that relation as an interaction, or a hermeneutic circle of the kind described by Paul Ricoeur between narrative and life, whereby the temporality of narrative and the temporality of life constantly modify each other. Such an account aims to make something of the discrepancy between time and narrative – to value the discrepancy for the understanding of temporality that it yields, rather than discount narrative temporality as a mere metaphor.

Chapter 7

Temporal Perspective: Narrative Futurity and the Distribution of Knowledge

The idea that the perspectival structure of fictional discourse is crucial for its representation of temporality finds an extended exploration if we change tradition from semantics, and the way that semantics has informed contemporary narratology, to the phenomenology of internal time-consciousness, and by extension, to phenomenological approaches to the temporality of literature. A foundational argument here is Roman Ingarden's discussion of temporal perspective in *The Cognition of the Literary Work of Art*, which explores the idea of temporal perspective in fiction as a special case of the more general phenomena of temporal perspective in the human experience of time. As a special case of time in general, it might seem as if this is not an account of the kind I have just described, that values the discrepancy between fictional, semiotic time on one hand and lived, experiential time on the other, and it is certainly true that much of Ingarden's argument emphasises the similarity between the concretisation or cognition of the literary work and the experience of time flow in general. Ingarden divides his analysis into two issues: the apprehension of the work during reading, and the cognition of the work after reading, and much of the similarity he establishes between reading and living belongs to the first of these questions. Much of this turns on the idea that, in reading, there is a quasi-present, or a part of the work that is 'vividly present to us', and although it need not be, this part of the work is often identical with the semantic unit of the sentence: the quasi-present of the reader is the present sentence. There are ways in which the present part of the work differs from the actual present moment of the reader in which it is embedded: the present of the reader is not a 'temporal point', Ingarden tells us, following Bergson, and the 'extension' of the reader's present can vary greatly, both in terms of the time referred to and the quantity of words or sentences that seem vividly present. But, on the whole, the experience of the present in reading is one of authentic time flow:

In the course of reading a work, it is always a new part or phase which is immediately vivid and present to the reader. Each phase passes from the state in which it was still unknown to the reader and announced itself only in a vague way, if at all, into the state of being already known but no longer actual or vividly present. (1973, 98)

The description of time flow here, like the semantic arguments above, emphasises the question of knowledge over time, so that events pass from a state of being 'still unknown', through the vivid and immediate present, into the realm of the 'already known'. There is, in fact, a general adherence to the vocabulary of the still unknown and the already known in Ingarden's discussion of the literary work of art, and a tendency to replace this terminology with that of 'past', 'present' and 'future' only when he turns his attention to the lived experience of time, as if this might be the basis for the distinction between the two: that in texts the dynamic flow is from the unknown to the known, whereas in life the flow is from the future to the past. Of course, the distinction cannot be as clearly drawn as that, but this general adherence does help to reduce the problems of confusing the future of a linguistic sequence with the future time to which it may refer. Whatever the overlap between these two vocabularies, of the unknown and the future, the vacillation between them helps to manage the simple fact that what is 'to come' in a discourse can be futural in a number of distinct senses, including the future of the linguistic sequence, future time to which that sequence refers, or a perspectivally determined future in which knowledge arrives from the future for a particular person involved in the narrative, but which may pertain to the past, or have existed all along for others: future words, future events and future knowledge.

Given this variety in the forms of futurity in a literary work, it follows that the idea of the vivid and immediate present must also take a number of forms, and we would expect this, in turn, to characterise the relationship between the present that we live and the present that takes place when we read. Ingarden speaks first of the reading activity itself:

The part of the work we are reading just now is immediately, vividly present to us because at just the moment of reading we are actively performing those signitive acts which constitute the meaning of the sentence (or group of sentences) in its concrete unfolding. (1973, 98)

This sentence might at first seem relatively modest in its scope. It claims that the vivid present consists in the active constitution of meaning in any moment of reading, but it does nothing to limit the scope of its two most indeterminate concepts – the 'moment' and the 'meaning of the sentence' – the first of which is of uncertain duration, and the second of which must hold within it the temporal reference of the sentence as well as its position in the linguistic sequence. This first attempt, to locate the vivid present in the reading activity itself, succeeds only in importing several different problems about the constitution of the present into an apparently circular claim that what is present is the presence of a signitive act. The second account of the vivid present refers us to the reverberation of sounds:

> It is also present to us because we vividly imagine that the stock of verbal sounds and the various phonetic formations and phenomena of higher order in the concrete details which appear one after the other are 'sounding in our ears'. (1973, 98)

Again, the apparent simplicity of still reverberating sound offers a straightforward account of vivid presence which is, at the same time, catastrophically complicated by its conjunction with 'phenomena of higher order', making it difficult to decide whether the concrete details in question are sounds, larger units such as words and sentences, or referents. Even at the phonetic level, the sentence seems unsure whether sounds are present or not since, if we only imagine these sounds, if they do not literally sound in our ears, their presence is also their absence. Both of these problems, the indissociability of phonetic from referential aspects of discourse, and the role of imagination in presence, lead Ingarden into a little crisis in the passage that follows, around the question of whether, in this vivid present, we are witnesses to language itself or to the objects and events to which language refers:

> The objectivities portrayed in the phase of the literary work of art present to us appear as clothed in concrete intuitive aspects. It is as if we were direct witnesses to what is just now happening in the objective stratum of the work, as well as to everything which appears in that phase in the other strata of the work. How can we be witnesses to the events portrayed in the work when, in dealing with a purely literary work, we do not actually perceive these objects and events in the strict sense of the word? This is a matter that demands special discussion. But such an analysis of the various possible modes of having consciousness of the objects with which we enter into relationship would far surpass our present investigation. In any case it is impossible to be satisfied with the stereotyped view that the reader simply 'imagines' the objects when he reads. One would at least have to say that there is a particular way of 'imagining' which makes the 'imagined' object present to us. (1973, 98–9)

There are two related elements of this crisis from which Ingarden wants to retreat. The first is the relationship between the objective stratum of the work, such as the sounds ringing in our ears, and all the other strata of the work, which are the 'concrete intuitive aspects' in which they seem to be clothed. We are direct witnesses to both of these: to words and their sounds, as well as to events and objects, despite the fact that we do not actually perceive those words and objects. There is some confusion here about what are objectivities and what are objects as we move from written words, which we do perceive as we read, to sounds ringing in our ears, which we 'vividly imagine', to events and objects that we imagine in a special way that makes them present to us. The second element of the crisis, which therefore emerges from the preliminary difficulty of isolating the objective stratum of the work, is this vague concept of the 'particular way of imagining', which seems to want to preserve the concept of presence despite the absence of its defining characteristic in actual perception: we witness without witnessing.

As it encounters its central problem, of stipulating the nature of presence in the apprehension of a literary work, Ingarden's argument is collapsing here into vagueness. In the description of time flow as the passing of the still unknown into immediate presence and on into the already known, his language becomes cluttered with the markers of provisionality, analogy and metaphoricity. The future announces itself 'only in a vague way' before distancing itself 'in a peculiar way' from the present, and the peculiarity of this movement causes Ingarden to reach repeatedly for provisional formulations ('one could say that', 'it appears to us', 'it is as if') and arguments of relative inadequacy ('it is impossible to be satisfied with the stereotyped view,' 'one would at least have to say that there is a particular way of imagining'). What is most important in this passage, however, is the need to preserve the notion of presence without the notion of actual perception, and for this task, Ingarden reaches for Husserl's terminology: 'Husserl speaks of a 'presentification' [Vergegenwartigung] which, though different from 'presentifying' [Gegenwartigung] which takes place during perception, is definitely related to it' (1973, 99). The distinction between presentification and presentifying is therefore the distinction between reading and perceiving, and the relation is one of similarity and difference. This might be thought of as a way of understanding the notion of a quasi-present, a term that Ingarden does not use, but which serves to indicate the present-like-ness of the immediate and vivid present in reading alongside the absence of actual perception. The basis for the distinction, however, is not elaborated here, and the only argument offered in this discussion is the fact that the present phase of reading differs from the parts we have already read by virtue of the fact that it is the focus of our present attention.

One of the interests of this apparently circular argument is that it favours the contrast of this immediate and present focus to the already read over the relation to the still unknown. 'That there really is such a presentification when we "imagine" the objects in the present phase of reading', he argues at the moment of introducing the concept, 'is seen most clearly when we compare the phase of the work present to us with the parts we have already read' (1973, 99). The notion of presentification, like that of presentifying, may not receive any elaboration in Ingarden's discussion, but it carries with it an active connotation, of making present, and this notion of activity extends also into the contrasting realm of the already read. This is what Ingarden refers to as the 'active memory', active in the sense that it does not consist in the recollection of all the words and sentences that have slipped into the past, but retains past meanings by compressing them into new and shortened forms. This process of abbreviation happens both consciously and unconsciously: consciously when a reader turns his (sic) attention back to the parts of the work already read, resulting in new actualisations of those parts in condensed form; and unconsciously, when these abbreviated meanings form as if on their own accord, without any special act of remembering, as the reader progresses. In both cases, these condensations of past meanings are responses to the temporal distance that forms between the present phase of a reading and the parts already read, and it follows, again with the insistence of a logical circle, that presentification, or the immediate and vivid present, is that which is neither distanced nor abbreviated in this way. If Ingarden chooses to verify presentification with reference to the already read, he does not, however, completely neglect the other horizon, of what is to come, and his account of time flow in the literary work of art depends also on Husserl's expression of the 'double horizon' of concretisation. Hence, in addition to the processes of active memory, we also need to contrast presentification with the parts of the work not yet read:

> In contrast to the immediate, vividly present phase of the work, we have those parts which the reader has not yet come to but which he is constantly approaching in the course of the reading. They too exist in some way for the reader, although in general he does not know them at all. Sometimes, because of the dynamics of the work, parts which the reader is approaching announce themselves with rather clear and definite features. Certain 'coming' events announce themselves in outline; sometimes several possibilities announce themselves at once. But only further reading can give us positive knowledge of whether and to what extent the events announcing themselves take place. (1973, 102–3)

There seems to be much less to say about the horizon of events to come, and certainly little that lies outside the category of the obvious:

that sometimes we can tell and sometimes we cannot tell what is going to take place, and we have to read on to find out for sure. The most interesting claim above is that events to come exist in some way for the reader, although he (this man who reads) generally does not know them at all. But this is not the already-there-ness of the future that I have associated with written narrative throughout my argument. It is rather the existence of a protention: a part of the vivid present that exists in that present as an expectation. For this reason, the category of the unexpected, the phenomenon of the narrative surprise, has a rather empty role in the argument about time flow and its relation to temporal perspective:

> 'Surprises', sometimes consciously prepared, are not without importance, especially for the aesthetic apprehension of the literary work of art: something appears in the objective stratum of the work, or in the other strata, which could not have been foreseen. Or else something which was prepared and expected does not occur. The preparation of such a surprise occurs through certain artistic means, by which something indicated in the text as possible and threatening suddenly does not happen at all but is replaced by its opposite. There are special artistic effects in such a surprise; and it is not without significance for the aesthetic apprehension of the work that these surprise phenomena be apprehended by the reader in their correct role, which is important for the development of the work. (1973, 103)

For my purposes this is an important passage, but nothing is more important than its failure to specify the importance of the unforeseen, or to apprehend the connection of the unexpected to the perspectival structure of a narrative. Perhaps it would be fairer to say that Ingarden recognises the importance of events to come for the completion of his account of time flow, without pursuing the question of the still unknown as a phenomenon of temporal perspective. So, on the positive side, we have the following account of time flow in the literary work of art:

> But independently of the way in which the coming parts of the work announce themselves to the reader and of what features of the work can and do so announce themselves, the reader is always aware of the phenomenon of progression to new parts or phases of the work and sometimes also of the constant decrease in the parts of the work which are still unknown. The phenomenon of the constant increase in the parts already read is also perceptible. That is what gives the process of reading the character of a movement which unfolds in a certain tempo and with a characteristic dynamism.
>
> The part of the work we are now reading is thus constantly surrounded by a double horizon (if we may use Husserl's expression here): (a) of the parts already read, which sink into the 'past' of the work, and (b) of those parts which have not yet been read and which are unknown up to the present moment. (1973, 103–4)

What is admirably clear in this account is the dynamic between past and future on one hand and 'already read' and 'still unknown' on the other, of a sequence of words, parts and phases on one hand and a sequence of events, non-events and discoveries on the other, in the phenomenon of progression. There is, in Ingarden's words, a 'polyphonic harmony' in the interaction of the different strata of a literary work which is absolutely dependent on the arrangement of its consecutive phases, so that the concretisation of a work, in all its aspects, is functionally dependent on the double horizon of the already read and the still unknown. But this is also the point at which Ingarden turns to the question of temporal perspective, which, in a literary work, is 'only a special case of "temporal perspective" in general', and therefore to the question of the relationship of the literary work of art and life, and when he does so, the future horizon, and the question of the still unknown, vanishes.

Ingarden begins his discussion of temporal perspective with a kind of dismissal of the future along the following lines: although in principle the phenomenal time of lived experience extends in two different directions, the concrete appearance of events takes place in the present moment, and this creates an asymmetry between, on one hand, the present moment and those temporal phases already experienced, and on the other, the temporal phases that are still to come. This asymmetry is the result of an essential emptiness and phenomenal vagueness of future time:

> The temporal phases of the approaching future, on the other hand, announce themselves either as empty temporal schemata which seem merely to be thought rather than being phenomenally present to us; or else, when we are expecting certain coming events, we imagine them in the form of only vaguely indicated qualities of the temporal phases. As a result of this phenomenal vagueness, a temporal phase which merely indicates itself qualitatively is not clearly and definitively integrated with phenomenal time. Usually, as soon as such a vaguely indicated temporal phase becomes the actual present moment, its qualitative determination is completely different from what it seemed in mere anticipation; and this is true even when the expected events have actually come about. (1973, 106)

In this way, on the grounds that an anticipation differs from what actually comes about, the future is banished from the discussion of temporal perspective. The consequences of this manoeuvre for what Ingarden will have to say about temporal perspective in the literary work are easily foreseeable: that the critical concept of temporal perspective will take as its object the relation of the present to the past. It may be that this is a justifiable reduction, perhaps even a simple consequence of what is generally described in philosophy as the ontological asymmetry of time, but it also brings into view the philosophical basis of a tendency in narratology and narrative theory to bracket the future. If it has been my contention in the previous chapter that there is, in possible worlds theory and cognitive narratology, a tendency to reduce the concept of epistemic modality by way of an exclusion of its futural meanings, there is here a similar reduction on the basis of a presentism that equates futurity in general with phenomenal vagueness. It is well known that Husserl's account of internal time-consciousness, for all of its emphasis on the notion of the present as a crossed structure of protentions and retentions, favours the notion of retention over protention for the same reasons, and therefore no surprise that his pupil, Ingarden, should also retreat from the future in the analysis of temporal perspective: that, despite the remarks cited above about the aesthetic importance of surprise, surprise should play no further part in the discussion. Ingarden, in fact, lists seven issues that give content to the notion of temporal perspective, which can be summarised as follows: (1) that temporal phases can seem shorter when they slip into the distance than they do in the present; (2) that the opposite can also be true, as, for example, in moments of extreme nervous tension, so that present experiences can seem much shorter than they do in later recollection; (3) that the dynamic properties of time as a process of becoming can be lost in recollection, when they appear as something complete; (4) that memory never succeeds in re-enacting perception, and that past events are inescapably recalled from a temporal 'point of view'; (5) that events sink further into the past, but that this sinking is not identical with the concept of temporal distance, which refers to the temporal aspect under which an event appears in recollection; (6) that events in the past necessarily change in recollection, and that the past is in this sense mutable; and (7) that there are expanded, detailed recollections and limited, abbreviated ones. These are the special phenomena of temporal perspective as they appear under temporal aspects (the temporal equivalents of the spatial aspects of material things when they are perceived visually) and they are all concerned with memory, or the relation of the past to the present.

As we would expect, this list of issues for general temporal perspective translates into a species of literary analysis entirely concerned with the relation of present to past events, where the horizon of the still unknown has dropped out of the picture. Ingarden's discussion is, in fact, mainly concerned with the feelings of temporal distance and proximity to past events that narrative is capable of producing as it shifts between perspectives in which our relation to events is indirect to those in which we feel like eyewitnesses. Part of this movement is generated from the interweaving of different time phases of events referred to and the time locus of narration itself, so that the relations of 'earlier' and 'later' are constantly deciphered in the apprehension of the 'whole abundance of manifestations of temporal perspective which unfold in the story', and which he follows in the opening chapter of Conrad's *Lord Jim*. Compared to the very detailed explorations of perspective which we find in 'point of view' analysis or in literary stylistics, or the highly organised readings of temporal order and duration in Genette's readings of Proust, Ingarden's reflections on these issues can seem unrewarding. On the other hand, there are important emphases in the ideas of temporal perspective that help to define the contribution that phenomenological approaches can make to the understanding of time flow in narrative, and which fall into three primary categories. The first of these contributions derives from the general emphasis placed on the reading process itself, and the way that this expands upon the temporal structure of represented events. Ingarden is careful to distinguish the two spheres involved in concretisation:

> On the one hand, the events and processes portrayed in the work appear under various phenomena of temporal perspective. On the other hand, temporal perspective also applies to the individual phases or parts of the whole work, or of its concretization, which have already been read. Thus there occurs a peculiar 'crossing' of the two applications of temporal perspective. (1973, 124)

These peculiar crossings between the linguistic sequence and the sequence of events to which it refers have to be observed by any narratology focused on the interaction of futurity and the still unknown in the experience of narrative time flow. The second contribution affirms the importance of an expanded notion of tense, or the need to understand tense structures in narrative at a level of discourse above the tense of verbs. Because the 'tense of the verb does not suffice to determine whether the portrayed events seem to lie in the past or in a special present' (1973, 125), Ingarden effectively displaces the notion of tense with the notion of perspective, and in so doing, offers a considerably more complicated account than notions of past or present tense are capable of comprehending. Like the notion of 'crossings', Ingarden regards these complicated relations between perspective and tense as fundamentally peculiar, as they have to be if a vivid present is to be represented in the past tense: 'The reader takes a peculiar recollective-perceptive attitude,' since 'the reader's return to the time of the described events allows him to observe these events, so to speak, from the same temporal phase in which they are developing' (1973, 126). Finally, we must remember that Ingarden took the step of dividing the discussion of temporal perspective into two projects – the cognition of the literary work during reading, and its cognition after reading – and that the entire discussion thus far has been concerned with the experience of time flow *during* reading. The third category of contribution comes from the rather abbreviated comments about the relationship between the apprehension of time during and after reading that close the discussion.

> It might be said that we know the work from all sides only at the moment in which we have finished reading and still have a vivid impression of the work . . . This aspect of the work has certain advantages over those we have in the course of the reading; it gives us, at least in principle, the whole work. We know there are no more parts to follow, that nothing is missing, which is, of course important for our understanding. In theory everything should have been explained at this point. (1973, 143)

It is probably apparent that this is a provisional argument ('it might be said', 'at least in principle', 'in theory'), soon to be retracted in favour of the position that this aspect 'does not render the work in any more adequate way than any earlier aspect'. The adequate rendering of a work, for Ingarden, consists in the combination of these two aspects of temporal perspective, and not in the choice between them, so that the actual apprehension of parts that are present during reading, the active memory of parts already read during reading, and the résumé of the whole work after reading, the final knowing which allows the reader to perform analytic and synthetic acts of apprehension, together comprise the cognition of the work. These three peculiarities – the peculiar crossings between events and parts, the peculiar recollective-perceptive attitude of perspective, and the combination of during and after – form a useful summary of the phenomenological legacy for a narratological approach to temporality.

It is well known that the critique of phenomenology, most obviously the readings of Husserl by Derrida, take the presentism of this kind of account, and its larger context of a metaphysics of presence, as its central concern. It is less often said that this is a critique of the bracketing of the future, the favouring of retention over protention, or the retreat from the still unknown, as enacted in deconstruction's preoccupation with the philosophy of futurity. But if deconstruction is a place where the concern for the future, all but absent in Husserl but central for Heidegger, is restored, this is not in evidence in the new narratologies, in cognitive semantics, or in possible worlds theories, and the question remains of what a theory of narrative would look like that tried to take seriously these three tenets – the crossings of spheres, the expansion of tense into temporal perspectives, and the joining of anticipation to retrospection – that have been extracted from Ingarden. To put it as concisely as possible, we need to observe that an expanded notion of the future tense which also joins retrospect to anticipation is, as was argued in the previous chapter, a structure that characterises written narrative in itself, and a process which combines waiting for things to happen with their already having taken place. This is paramount to saying that any analysis that hopes to account for time flow in discourse must not limit itself to the time line on which progress is simply an actualisation of future events in the present, but must project on to this temporal axis the question of perspective, and to understand flow in this expanded sense, as the distribution of knowledge across time.

PART IV
The Unforeseeable in Fictional Form

Chapter 8

Maximum Peripeteia: Reversal of Fortune and the Rhetoric of Temporal Doubling

In *Fingersmith*, by Sarah Waters, something very unexpected happens. It happens at the end of Part One, after six chapters, about one-third of the way through the novel, and it turns everything upside down. We had thought that Sue Trinder, our narrator, was part of a plot to cheat an heiress out of her fortune by having her committed to a mental asylum, but in fact the heiress, Maud, was also part of a plot, of which we knew nothing, to have Sue locked up in the madhouse. The scene in which Sue travels to the asylum with her partner in crime Richard to commit Maud, only to be handed over herself to the doctors by Richard and Maud, presents one of those absolutely unpredictable moments on which mystery fiction turns: an unexpected event that arrives from the future, which cancels everything we had thought to be the case and replaces everything we expected to happen.

But does it arrive from the future? Its unexpectedness is organised by the perspectival structure of the novel and by the distribution of information that this structure entails, because we only know what Sue knows, and access to information possessed by other characters is withheld. It is true that, as we read through Part One, the asylum event has not happened yet, but its unexpectedness is the function of what we do not yet know more than it is the function of what has not yet happened. To put it another way, what has not yet happened, in the case of an unexpected event, is knowledge of something, and the unexpected event is one that coincides with the arrival of this knowledge. All events can be said to arrive from the future, but very few arrive unannounced, unanticipated, or without the trailer of expectation, and when they do they reveal something about the past: that there has been a secret, or a failure, or an absence of knowledge in the prehistory of the event. One of the primary meanings of the word *event*, especially as it is used in contemporary philosophy, is that it is unexpected: that eventhood entails surprise, unpredictability or the absence of anticipation, and that events that we expect lack significance in proportion to the foreknowledge we have of them. One of the ways of understanding the temporality of fictional narrative is through the way that it organises expectation by controlling the distribution of knowledge across time, and specifically, the way that it produces experiences of expectation and surprise for a reader. But any attempt to understand this has to address itself to a question as much about truth as about time; that is, address itself to the question of what we do not yet know as much as what has not yet taken place.

Questions of who knows what and when are particularly important to novels like *Fingersmith*, which unfold as a series of deceptions and revelations, but even in relatively straightforward cases such as this, the answers are not simple. Sue's narrative in Part One is, after all, a discourse that reproduces her own original state of ignorance so that the reader shares her experience and her surprise, believing that she is conning Maud and subsequently discovering that she is herself the dupe. But because she narrates after the event, and therefore knows as she narrates what she did not know, the proximity between narrator and reader is undone by the revelation, and we think of Sue what Sue thinks of Maud at the moment of realisation: 'That bitch knew everything. She had been in on it from the start' (2003, 175). Something analogous to the discovery that Sue has been tricked takes place at a metanarrative level, in the relationship between the narrator and the reader, as the careful preparation of the unexpected comes into view. There are several reasons to think of this as a metanarrative effect, and they are generally concerned with the distribution of knowledge over time, or of who knows what and when. In the first place, the content level of the story seems to be working as a kind of allegory for something which is inherent in first person narrative voice; namely, the split of a single person into two – Sue the narrator and Sue the narrated, one of whom knows what is going to happen and the other who does not know. This distribution of knowledge, the division of knowing and not knowing, is repeated in the relationship between Sue and Maud, so that Sue's discovery of Maud's deception dramatises, or perhaps constitutes, our discovery of the truth of what our narrator has known all along. That a first person narrator might withhold subsequent discoveries or realisations cannot be thought of as an unusual predicament in narrative, but there are two observations to be drawn from it, the first of which applies to the conduct of this particular narrative while the second points to something common to all narrative sequences. This particular narrative has a special interest in the similarity, and indeed interchangeability, of Sue and Maud which results from the reciprocity of two plots of mistaken

identity, in which one character is passed off as the other. The convergence of Sue and Maud in Part One of *Fingersmith* encodes in a dramatised relationship, more than most narratives would, the undramatised
relation between a narrator and an external reader, between who writes
and who is written, or who controls and who is controlled, through its
commingling of Sue and Maud's identities. This is what is meant by the
notion of a metanarrative allegory at work in the novel: that for all of its
particularity in this plot, there is a basic question for narrative that is
enacted by the relationship of Sue and Maud about the trade-off
between suspense and irony that inheres in all narrative sequences.

We accept, as a matter of convention, the notion that narrators will
not tell all from the start, or that they will tell in a manner that remains
faithful to the experiential sequence they purport to represent. We might
accept here, for example, that Sue the narrator (Sue 2) should reproduce
for us the experience of not knowing that Sue the narrated (Sue 1) supposedly lived through. If the difference between Sue 1 and Sue 2 is one
of temporal location, before and after the event, what I have been suggesting in the paragraph above is that the relationship between Sue 1
and Sue 2 is encoded in the relationship between Sue and Maud which,
because of a plot based in the physical similarity of Sue and Maud, can
resonate with suggestions that they are, in fact, like Sue 1 and Sue 2, the
same person, or different facets of the same person. The importance of
these resonances is that they point something out about the convention
we have accepted, particularly for cases of first person narration, that
narrators might not tell all from the start, because Sue-and-Maud offers
a spatialised or synchronic analogue of a relationship that is fundamentally temporal and diachronic: Sue-and-Maud stands in the place of Sue
1–then-Sue 2. The reason that we might view this as a way of pointing
out something about the convention of first person narration, perhaps
the structure of recollection in general, is that the relation Sue-and-
Maud encodes the co-presence of Sue 1 and Sue 2, or the presence of the
Sue that knows already what is to come, in every narrative sentence or
temporal phase that makes up the prehistory of the unexpected event.
Again, it might be thought that this is simply to be accepted as the necessary condition of the production of suspense – Sue 2 may be structur-
ally present as the voice that recollects, as the present part of the tense
relation between the present time of the utterance and the past time to
which it refers – but it is a voice that must not divulge what it knows
in the service of the story. It may be that Maud in some way represents
that knowledge to come in the present, but a first-time reader does not
know that yet, and to identify her in this way is nothing more than a
facet of the general revision that takes place when the reader comes to

know. We are, of course, stuck here between two perspectives which, recalling Ingarden's discussion in the previous chapter, pertain to the cognition of the work during reading and the cognition of the work after reading, and there is a commonsense view that would hold these two perspectives apart: that there is, on one hand, the question of what we know during reading, and on the other what we know after reading, and we should not confuse the two by suggesting that the after reading is somehow present in the during reading. But it is exactly this opposition, of presence and retrospection, and the idea of presence as future (and therefore unavailable) retrospection that narratives, even those with the most straightforward and conventional temporal structures, seem to place in question. This is clear in the resistance that even the most conventional temporal structures in narrative generate in relation to the categories that try to analyse them, even when those categories seem to underpin the most fundamental assumptions we hold about time, such as the distinction between presence and retrospection. We might say that the tense structure of this narrative, by joining the time of the utterance to the time of events to which it refers, turns presence into retrospection and retrospection into presence. But we need also to qualify immediately the alignment we have just made between Ingarden's cognition during reading and cognition after reading with presence and retrospection in general, since the latter is strictly speaking a perspective reached when there are no more parts to come, and the unexpected event we are concerned with in *Fingersmith* is not an ending. The interplay of during and after, in other words, is one particular dynamic of presence and retrospection, but is by no means the only one, and we should really regard this event, at the end of Part One, as part of the interplay that is internal to the category of cognition *during* reading, between the already known and the still unknown. The finality of an ending is not the essential feature of the suture of presence and retrospection, in the sense that the moving now of reading transforms presence into retrospection at every stage in the process of reading, as it passes from attention into memory, where that presence was always quasi-presence, since it was the experience of somebody else's retrospection in the first place.

Let us return, then, to the idea that Sue and Maud enact something about narrative convention, about the distribution of knowledge in narrative and, in the process, form a metanarrative commentary upon the relationship between a writer and a reader. A starting point here might be the words 'plot' and 'story', and the double-reference that these have from the novel's beginning to lies, schemes and deceptions on one hand and to narrative structures and books on the other. When Gentleman first proposes his deception of Maud and her father, his plan is expressed as a story:

> 'So, my son,' he said. 'What's the story?'
> Gentleman looked up.
> 'The story,' he said. 'The story is this.' He took out a card, and laid it face-up, on the table. It was the King of diamonds. 'Imagine a man,' he said, as he did it. 'An old man – a wise man, in his own way – a gentleman scholar, in fact; but with curious habits. He lives in a certain out-of-the-way kind of village, some miles from London – never mind just where, just now. He has a great room filled with books and prints, and cares for nothing but for them and for the work he is compiling – let's call it a dictionary. It is a dictionary of all his books . . . ' (2003, 23)

There are two elements in this description that establish the relationship between the plot as a planned deception and the question of books in general. The first is that the story as plan is substitutable for the story as a fictional narrative, to be imagined in a conventional storytelling situation, with a hot drink around the fire, so that the construction of the internal story as a plot stands as an emblem for the novel as a whole – for the story that we are reading – and to this effect belong the many uses of the words 'story' and 'plot' in the opening chapters of the novel. The second is the presence of books within the story, the great quantity of books at Briar, and what they mean about its inhabitants, for a scholar who is 'wise in his own way', living in an 'out-of-the-way' village, and who cares for nothing but for them' (2003, 23). There is a certain connection between the two elements, since the detachment from the world connoted by the love of books makes the plot, as dastardly plan, more likely to succeed. Similarly, Maud's bookishness is repeatedly offered as an explanation of her dupable character, and her similarity to a 'girl in a story' (2003, 70) is also how Sue understands the determination of her future: 'For though I knew her fate – though I knew it so well, I was helping to make it! – perhaps I knew it rather in the way you might know the fate of a person in a story or a play' (2003, 96). We can, in fact, understand many of the novel's details as working in the service of this connection between plots and books, the difference between making a plot and being its victim, and the question of knowing what is going to happen. As Gentleman sets out his story, in the extract cited, he lays a playing card on the table, in order to lend the gravity of fate to the plot he concocts, and this too functions to marshal the story's details into the service of a metanarrative commentary about who knows what in the story at large: 'Should you like to know your future, miss?' Sue asks Maud later at Briar; 'Did you know you can read it from how the cards fall?' (2003, 99). In this later scene, as Sue lays out Maud's past, present and future from a sprung pack, the question of who is in the story and who is writing it, of who controls the story and who is subject to its fatalism, seems primarily to make us laugh at what Maud does not know, and only in retrospect, or on a second reading, to realise the irony of who knows what and when, and who is in control of the story. The whole dynamic of knowing and not knowing, of controlling and being controlled, is imaged here as a relationship between an author and a character, but in this set of associations lies a clue of what is to come: Sue does not know how to read.

Clues of this kind, in fact, abound in the relationship between Sue and Maud, and are an important source of structure for the kind of narrative that places its moment of maximum peripeteia not at the end of the story but at an early stage. If, as I argued above, the relationship between knowing and now knowing is somehow encoded in the tense structure of the narrative and further emblematised in the relationship between Sue and Maud, we cannot regard the reversal of expectations as one that takes place in the relationship between cognition during and cognition after reading. The novel's structure is rather one of constant realisation and revision of the significance of narrated events, both at the level of a series of renarrations of the events initially narrated by Sue, and in the revision of single details when new light is shed by revelations and disclosures.

> The facts and objects retained in active memory during reading are constantly changing [Ingarden says], not simply because the multiplicity of facts portrayed keeps growing, but also, as the reading progresses, other processes, events, or characters often assume a significance for the reader which is different from the significance they seem to have in the earlier parts. (Ingarden 1973, 102)

For this reason we have to recall certain events to the active memory while we read whose significance has been revealed, clarified or altered by later events. This may entail the wholesale revision of the sequence of events thus far, as when we reassess Sue's reliability as a narrator in the light of her ignorance of the truth, or of a more local detail, as when we recognise that Maud's preference for a worn-out dress before the trip to the madhouse was part of a plot to pass herself off as a servant and Sue as a lady. These are the most pedestrian of narrative effects as they work in the service of mystery. But we also need to think of the process of continuous revision as part of the basic interplay between the arrival of the future and the arrival of knowledge in fictional time flow, or, as Wayne Booth has it, the author's choice of whether to purchase mystery at the expense of irony:

As in most novels, whatever steps are taken to mystify inevitably decrease the dramatic irony, and, whenever dramatic irony is increased by telling the reader secrets the characters have not yet suspected, mystery is inevitably destroyed . . . And we all find that on second reading we discover new intensities of dramatic irony resulting from the complete loss of mystery. (Booth 1961, 255)

From this point of view, the metacommentary involving ideas about plotting, stories, fate and the knowability of the future are all sacrificed to mystery, deferred until the moment of revision or apprehended only on a second reading. These secrets, which the author might tell the reader and thereby destroy mystery, might be thought unavailable in a first person narrative because a narrator cannot tell a reader what they themselves do not know. In fact, the first person narrative simply temporalises the work of disclosing secrets, so that the narrator is the character speaking from a position of subsequent knowledge; the complementarity between the perspectives of knowledge and ignorance is therefore all the tighter by virtue of being bound together in the single person, and the tensed voice, of the narrator. If we are going to think in terms of a trade-off between irony and suspense, therefore, it must be in terms of the rigour with which the narrator excludes the narrative present from the quasi-present of narrated events, since mystery and suspense would be easily destroyed by any kind of proleptic visitation of the time locus of narration. Within this structure, the idea of a clue is suspended between two time zones as a detail that must await the confirmation of its significance as an indication of what is to come; it is an anticipation which must be perceived only in retrospect lest it destroys the structure of suspense in which it functions. By extension, the idea of a metanarrative clue functions as a commentary on the reading process itself that must remain unperceived until after the unfolding of that process. In contrast to the secret jokes that Booth describes as taking place between readers and a silent author, these ones seem to take place silently between an author and herself, at least until they can be perceived in hindsight.

The clue or hint, as a narrative element apparently made up of both the presence and absence of concrete expectation, is not simply a question of the *not yet* of knowledge to come. Several other factors must be taken into consideration if we are to think beyond the position that Peter Brooks describes as a wish to shout 'Wait! For God's sake wait.' We need, for example, to acknowledge, with Ingarden, Booth, Barthes, Brooks and many others, that the clue or hint is not an objectivity in the text so much as a part of the hermeneutic process of a given reader, and that it is necessary not only to distinguish different levels of readerly competence (Booth speaks of the 'perceptive reader') but also to highlight the difficulty of distinguishing the clue from what Tomachevsky calls the 'motivation' of narrative details, and therefore from the general inferential and anticipatory activity of given readers. Some readers might have guessed that, in a plot that hinges on the similarity and exchange of two women, there was a reversal to come, or inferred from the system of clues, the playing cards, the interplay of readers and writers the event to come. In addition to the general generic expectation, which depends upon the reader's knowing in advance that this is a mystery fiction, and that the genre characteristically makes use of surprise, there is a set of specific expectations that arise in relation to heiresses and plotting penniless gentlemen that may well inform the hermeneutic processes of given readers. The determination of expectation in the reading process is, in other words, a much broader matter than the textual system of narrative plotting and perspectival structure; the expectations that a reader brings to a fiction like *Fingersmith* are not only textually produced, but depend on an indeterminate quantity of surrounding information of genre, of literary history, and of the nature of fiction more generally. This very broad context for the discussion of the hermeneutic process is what Jauss attempted to describe as the 'horizon of expectation', a notion that attempts to encompass three enormous domains of determining knowledge:

> First, through familiar norms or the immanent poetics of the genre; second, through the implicit relationships to familiar works of the literary-historical surroundings; and third, through the opposition between fiction and reality, between the poetic and the practical function of language, which is always available to the reflective reader during the reading as a possibility of comparison. (Jauss 1982, 24)

The problems of this notion have been widely discussed (Holub 1984, 60–3; Iser 1978, 111–12), often with specific reference to the problems of its relation to the phenomenological 'horizon', as discussed by Husserl, or the 'double horizon' of reading that we traced in Ingarden in the previous chapter. These latter meanings of 'horizon' are concerned with the constitution of the present, in life for Husserl and in reading for Ingarden, as a structure of protentions and retentions. Jauss's notion, on the other hand, is literary-historical and attempts to describe the historical formation of discourses, of generic knowledge and intertextual relations that hangs over hermeneutic activity. We might, according to this, simply know that *Fingersmith* is a mystery and therefore carry a generalised expectation of reversal and surprise through Sue's narrative, and equally we might know its specific similarity to Wilkie Collins's novel of 1859, *The Woman in White*, in which something very unexpected happens, the plot of which involves a striking resemblance between Laura Fairlie and Anne Catherick, the plotting of Sir Percival Glyde to rob Laura of her fortune, and the committing of Laura to a mental asylum as Anne. There is, on one hand, a general guide to unexpected events in *Fingersmith*, in the familiar forms and immanent poetics of mystery fiction in general, and an implicit relationship with a strikingly similar novel, and the degree of knowledge of these sources therefore functions as a spectrum of individual readers located somewhere between the ignorance and aware- ness. No matter how hard Jauss tried to formulate the 'horizon of expec- tation' in collective or historical terms, as a shared horizon, the idea of expectation in the actual reading process seemed indissociable from this individualistic, psychologistic and unquantifiable character in the expec- tation of given readers. Likewise, his attempts to rescue the notion of expectation from the inanities of individual reader-responses caused him to argue that the general formation of the horizon of expectations was, in fact, reconstructable from textual evidence, or properties of the object being read, and this not only seemed to contradict the basic premise of hermeneutics (that it is the study of the reading process and the factors involved in sense-making), but also to involve him in an inescapable logical circle, described by Holub in this way:

> As long as he insists on the possibility of a 'reconstruction of the horizon of expectations' and sets out to accomplish this reconstruction with evidence or signals from the works themselves, he is going to be measuring the effect or impact of works against a horizon that is abstracted from those works. (Holub 1984, 62)

It is easy to see here that the idea of generic expectation loses all utility as a concept if the concept itself has to be reconstructed from the object to which those expectations might apply. The generic expectations that might be brought to a reading of *Fingersmith*, for example, are neces- sarily established in advance of a reading and represent traits of a larger set which may or may not be discovered in that reading. If the horizon of expectation cannot account for the expectations of a given reader, and cannot be reconstructed from the textual signals of a given text, it is difficult to see what the positive content of these expectations might amount to in the cognition of the literary work, or to see what analytical purchase the concept could have on the reading process. We encounter the tension between the objectivity of the text and the subjectivity of the reading process in two different ways, first because it is undecidable whether clues and hints are textual features or part of the hermeneutic process, and second because expectation is suspended between collective and individual cognitive conditions, which, in terms of knowing what is to come, is the gap between the *it anticipates* of textual signals and the *I anticipate* of my individual reading process.

The textual signals that we think of as clues seem more problematic, in this respect, than the perspectival determinants of anticipation. The physical similarity of Sue and Maud shouts louder to the reader who has also read *The Woman in White* than to the reader who is working with generic expectations alone, whereas the perspectival aspects of expectation are more obviously internal to the text, and so are at work on any reader. Perspectival structures are thus more determining of the reading experience, and less variable from reader to reader. This is so even when perspectival structures are analysed alongside the more variable factors of expectation that come from generic or intertextual knowledge, so that even the reader more alert to clues and foreshadowings, whether Booth's 'more perceptive reader' or the Wilkie Collins fan, can anticipate only within the particular constraints of a narrative's distribution of information and knowledge across time. If Jauss's notion of the horizon of expectation, for all its efforts to collectivise, seemed to open the study of expectation up to an uncontrolled plurality of factors and an irreducible diversity of readers, the notion of perspectival structure offers some basis for the reunification of the readership and of the reading experience. The unexpected event in *Fingersmith*, for example, depends upon the preparation of an incorrect expectation or mistaken inference on the part of the readership as a whole, and the basis of this preparation is the control of knowledge. Booth holds that mystery is destroyed whenever dramatic irony is increased, and that dramatic irony is increased by telling the reader secrets, but this trade-off can also be exploited for the creation of false expectations. It is important to the conduct of Sue's narrative, for example, that dramatic irony works against Maud, in the sense that the knowledge we have of Gentleman's plot distances us from Maud, giving everything that happens to her after Sue's arrival the double significance of how it appears to her and how we know it to figure in the plot, in the light of what we know that she does not. Even if, in this predicament, we bring generic expectations of peripeteia to the experience, our anticipations are carefully led away from the actual reversal to come. There is a technical bonding of a reader to both Sue and Gentleman entailed in the information we share, but the expectation that the plot might not proceed as planned, or that this three-way bond might be betrayed, is more obviously generated by the love affair which takes place between Sue and Maud as Sue prepares the innocent Maud for marriage; the proximity of sex and love between Maud and Sue threatens to displace the proximity of the accomplices, and an avenue of anticipation is opened up around the question of whether Sue will go through with the deception. The fundamental device in the creation of surprise is the preparation of a different surprise, so that one possible distribution of knowledge (we know, Maud is deceived) generates anticipations that distract from what is to come, like a structural red herring. When we speak of irony in novels like this, or of the sharing of secrets between reader and narrator, perhaps even reader and silent author, we need to account for the pseudo-dramatic irony encountered during reading, which generates an array of false expectations, anticipations, hopes and fears, as well as the linear irony, according to which we look back and understand after the event in the light of what we did not know. From this point of view, the simple trade-off described by Booth between dramatic irony and suspense is too simple, because it understands dramatic irony as a reader's possession of true knowledge not yet suspected by a character which prevents mystery, where, in fact, mystery is often constructed around the realisation that our secrets are false.

Again we witness a collision between time and truth. The idea of dramatic irony as Booth understands it, as the destruction of suspense, is clearly at work, but in time, it turns out to be false. It is, in fact, difficult to keep the concept of dramatic irony apart from the question of time, because questions of what we know and do not know in fiction are inextricable from questions of what is going to happen and what we think is going to happen. The most important secret that a narrator can reveal to a reader, the secret that will most distance the reader from a character, is the secret of what is to come, and even if it is not delivered directly, as it is, for example, in prolepsis, any information possessed by the reader and not shared by a character will partake in some way of that secret. As the revelation of future events out of turn, prolepsis therefore offers a significant resource for the description of crossovers between time and truth in narrative, or of the distribution of information, truth or certainty over time in the arrangement of a plot. If, in third person narrative, prolepsis gives access to a future which is inaccessible to characters, the flashforward is godlike in its perspective, but in first person narrative the effect is considerably more mundane. For all the atmosphere of experimentation that surrounds the discussion of prolepsis, it is worth remembering, with Genette, that in the first person narrative voice prolepsis is structural:

> The 'first person' narrative lends itself better than any other to anticipation, by the very fact of its avowedly retrospective character, which authorizes the narrator to allude to the future and in particular to his present situation for those to some extent form part of his role. (Genette 1983, 67)

If the quasi-present is the time locus of narrated events, the future is already present in it by virtue of the fact that those events are viewed retrospectively from a 'present situation' in relation to which narrated events are past. As a matter of convention, first person narratives tend to move between these two presents and so to anticipate constantly the future time of the act of narration. It may be true that all knowledge will partake in some way of knowledge of the future, or of the secret of what is to come, and therefore that dramatic irony might destroy suspense, but when dramatic irony begins to merge into the category of prolepsis the proposition begins to look tautological, since knowledge of the future is self-evidently destructive of suspense if suspense is the state of not knowing the future. As a matter of convention, then, first person narratives destroy suspense, or can only sustain it, as I suggested earlier, in proportion to the rigour with which they exclude the present situation of narration from the story. *Fingersmith*, for example, systematically excludes the knowledge of Sue 2, the narrator, from the account of events even though it is structural in the retrospect of the voice, but does not eliminate reference to the temporal gap altogether:

> And then there came the morning when we learned he was coming back. It was an ordinary morning, except that Maud had woken and rubbed her face, and winced. – Perhaps that was what they call a premonition. I only thought that later, though. At the time, I saw her chafing her cheek and said, 'What's the matter?' (2003, 96)

This is a relatively unusual moment in so far as it refers to a thought that occurred later, and therefore relaxes the rigorous exclusion of events and perspectives to come. There are various points of temporal reference involved in this scene – a background of ordinary mornings, this specific morning on which 'we learned he [Gentleman] was coming back', a specific moment when Maud had woken in pain, and a later thought that this might have been a premonition. There is a sense in which 'later' and 'at the time' flaunt the temporal distance of the narrative voice, but the time of narration, the 'now' of the narrator's present situation, remains unmarked. Like prediction in general, it is one thing to identify a premonition at the time and something far less impressive to identify it as a premonition later, when something awful has happened, but that is what our narrator is doing here: pointing out that something trivial came to seem later like a foreshadow of something important. But what does 'later' mean here, and of what is this apparently trivial pain a premonition? The time referred to by 'later' in 'I only thought that later', though it must take place some time after the morning in question and before the moment of narration, is indeterminate, as is the question of whether that thought is continuous with, still the case in, the moment of narration or not. We have a case here of what Herman calls 'fuzzy temporal ordering' or 'temporal indefiniteness', and which Genette discusses as 'unplaceable' or (to Herman's disapproval) 'timeless' events. The question of what 'later' refers to is unanswerable here, and in the absence of an answer, we cannot decide if it represents some middle point between narration and narrated time, or a teleological perspective from which the narration emanates. At any rate, if prolepsis takes place in this extract, it does so only vaguely, referring forward to an unplaceable event that cannot be fully discerned, and we are positioned ambiguously between expectation and foreknowledge, between the future we expect at this point and the one that actually comes about. The expectation that Maud will be duped acts as an alibi, distraction from or preparation for the actual revelation to come, and the ambiguity of this proleptic flash therefore functions in the structure of false irony and irony that the narrative strings out in time, in the service of suspense. The fuzzy temporal position of this flashforward, in other words, is part of the rigour with which this particular narrative excludes perspectives from the time locus of narration, despite what Genette says about the inherent authority of first person narrators to comment on present situation, and at the same time making us think that we have glimpses of the future we expect. Prolepsis, from this point of view, is the device that offers an excursion into the secret knowledge that characters do not possess about present events, but the fuzzy flashforward allows prolepsis to operate in the production of either irony or suspense.

The relationship between irony and temporality has been addressed in numerous ways by literary criticism throughout its history. Kermode points out that peripeteia, for example, has often been understood as a temporalisation of irony:

> The story that proceeded very simply to its obviously predestined end would be much nearer myth than novel or drama. Peripeteia, which has been called the equivalent, in narrative, of irony in rhetoric, is present in every story of the least structural sophistication. Now peripeteia depends upon our confidence of the end; it is a disconfirmation followed by a consonance; the interest of having our expectations falsified is obviously related to our wish to reach the discovery or recognition by an unexpected and instructive route. (Kermode 2000, 18)

If irony is the reversal of surface appearances, or the secret meaning of events and utterances, peripeteia is the enactment of that reversal, or the disclosure of those secrets, in time. Kermode's view of peripeteia as a mark of structural sophistication, however, is not an obvious or necessary judgement on the value of the unexpected and instructive route to discovery. Booth claims, for example, that it is 'a commonplace of our criticism that significant literature arouses suspense not about the "what" but about the "how"', and that the mystification on which unexpected reversals turn 'has been mastered by so many second-rate writers that her [Austen's] efforts at mystification seem second-rate' (Booth 1961, 255). In a seminal essay on the relationship of irony and temporality, Paul de Man argues that the tendency to subsume the discussion of rhetorical tropes in questions of literary value impedes the progress of investigations: 'One of the main difficulties that still hamper these investigations stems from the association of rhetorical terms with value judgements that blur distinctions and hide the real structures' (De Man 1983, 188). Kermode's discussion of peripeteia is unashamedly focused on the value of upsetting naïve and rigid expectations, and on the value of literature capable of departure from a known paradigm:

> The degree of rigidity is a matter of profound interest in the study of literary fictions. As an extreme case you will find some novel, probably contemporary with yourself, in which the departure from a basic paradigm, the peripeteia in the sense I am now giving it, seems to begin with the first sentence. The schematic expectations of the reader are discouraged immediately. Since by definition one seeks the maximum peripeteia (in this extended sense) in the fiction of one's own time, the best instance I can give is from Alain Robbe-Grillet. (2000, 19)

We have moved away here from the idea of an unexpected ending, the expectation of which would be established in the progress of the fiction, to an expectation in place from the start, and which is capable of being demolished at the start. The 'maximum peripeteia' in this sense, is the maximal deviation of a contemporary fiction from the schematic expectations that are in place before reading, and one seeks this maximum from the fiction of one's own time, presumably because, if it had happened before, the paradigm that governs these expectations might already be altered. This is, for Kermode, partly a question of generic expectation, and of what constitutes 'a "story" in the traditional sense of the word', but it is also, in his discussion of Robbe-Grillet, that the 'time of the novel is not related to any exterior norm of time' and the fact that the story moves forward 'without reference to "real" time, or to the paradigms of real time familiar from conventional novels' (2000, 20). Against this melange of literary and more general expectations surrounding temporality, books make their own 'unexpected, unexpectable designs' and, in doing so, they stake their claims to modernity by degrees of unconventionality, originality and contempt for paradigm and expectation. The argument about value is never really concealed in this account of Robbe-Grillet, Sartre and Camus, and less so when Kermode turns attention to Dostoevsky's *The Idiot*, a novel 'which has the advantage of being universally regarded as a remarkable master-piece' and which 'abounds in surprising things' (2000, 22):

> All these are novels which most of us would agree (and it is by a consensus of this kind only that these matters, quite rightly, are determined) to be at least very good. They represent in varying degrees that falsification of simple expectations as to the structure of a future which constitutes peripeteia. (2000, 23)

These are novels determined by consensus to be good, and they are novels which falsify expectations, and from this conjunction we can assume at least that novels which contain peripeteia are not excluded from great-ness, and at most that novels are good because they challenge simple expectations. What, then, should we make of Booth's view of the unex-pected as the mark of second-rate fiction, or of Paul de Man's argument that value judgements 'hide the real structures' of rhetorical figures? One possible answer to the first question is that there are two distinct types of expectation involved in the discussion, the first being determined by aspects of a text such as perspectival structure, the presence or absence of prolepsis, clues and hints, while the second is a broader expectation of genre or fiction or literature in general determined by established para-digms and historical formations. Perspectival expectation, then, might be thought to underlie Booth's view of mystification at the expense of irony as the marker of the second-rate, and the more general aesthetic expectation to underlie Kermode's wish to link the falsification of expec-tations to sophisticated or great literature. Though the distinction seems important, the answer is not, in fact, as tidy as this, and it seems impor-tant to recognise that Kermode's discussion moves between perspectival and aesthetic senses of expectation and peripeteia without making the distinction, so that the unexpected and unexpectable designs of literary fictions can refer to trivial things concerned with not knowing what is going to happen, or to significant things about the way that literature challenges simple expectations about stories or about the nature of time. It is not, then, that there is a second-rate kind of peripeteia mastered by writers of genre fiction and controlled through perspectival structures, and a valuable kind that governs the originality of masterpieces, but varying degrees of peripeteia from simple disconfirmations to refigura-tions of time.

Perhaps de Man is right to think that the analysis of irony is better off without the clutter of value judgements, and that our task should be to understand but not to evaluate the structures of literature. His own argument about the relationship of irony to temporality is concerned at first with poetry, but its philosophical scope makes it relevant to our problem here of the tension between knowing and waiting in the apprehension of a narrative. I claimed earlier that, in *Fingersmith*, the relationship between Maud and Sue was a kind of allegory for the relationship between knowing and not knowing what is going to happen, or to put it another way, an allegory of the irony of the truth that will emerge. De Man's argument is about the relationship between these tropes, allegory and irony, and the role that temporality plays in the understanding of their structure. The question of value arises, in the first place, because, in the latter half of the eighteenth century, the term 'allegory' was supplanted by the term 'symbol' on the basis of a lot of spurious ideas and suppositions about the infinite suggestivity and the 'intimate unity between the image that rises up before the senses and the supersensory totality that the image suggests' (1983, 189). These were the qualities that made art great, and that established the superiority of symbol over allegory as a commonplace of literary taste. For de Man, this unity of an image and the totality for which it stands is part of a more general effort to unify subject and object, and in particular, an effort to think of the subject, or the self, as having the stability of natural objects. Behind the mere valorisation of symbol over allegory is a philosophical stance on selfhood aiming to extract the subject from temporal flux, spatialising the subject–object relation in a moment of simultaneity:

> In the world of symbol it would be possible for the image to coincide with the substance, since the substance and its representation do not differ in their being but only in their extension: they are part and whole of the same set of categories. Their relationship is one of simultaneity, which, in truth, is spatial in kind, and in which the intervention of time is merely a matter of contingency, whereas, in the world of allegory, time is the originary constitutive category. (1983, 207)

In this dichotomy between space and time, de Man finds, on the one hand, an illusory identification between the self and the non-self, and on the other, a kind of language that constantly designates a distance from its own origins. Unlike 'symbol', the tropes of allegory and irony are, according to de Man, definitely not organic. Rather than posit some kind of simultaneity between image and totality, these are tropes founded in and constituted by temporality, in the sense that the allegorical sign points to some previous sign with which it never coincides, since 'it is of the essence of this previous sign to be pure anteriority'

(1983, 207). This is a typical argument for de Man, who likes to translate already huge abstractions, like symbol and allegory, into even more abstract philosophical oppositions, like the opposition of time and space, which in turn can be mapped on to an opposition between illusory identifications with and the painful recognition of the non-self. De Man's arguments often 'discover' that the oppositions they have established in fact turn out to be unsupportable, but the demonstration rarely reflects badly on the cavalier translations performed by de Man's own discussion, and points instead to some unanalysed tension in the critical terminology, if not the rhetorical structure itself. If this sounds like a negative assessment of the argumentative strategy, it also needs to be recognised that de Man's untheorised confusion between critical arguments and the performance of rhetorical figures themselves is capable of some complex formulations that are unavailable to critics who assume an unproblematic separation of the subject and the object. The formulations towards which de Man progresses in 'The Rhetoric of Temporality' capture effectively the complexities of the basic structures of ignorance and reversal, irony and allegory, which inhabit the most straightforward fictional instances of the unexpected.

This movement is followed by de Man's discussion of irony and allegory in so far as he first translates these tropes into abstract oppositions, then has trouble with the oppositions, and then locates the trouble in the tropes themselves. Hence, irony and allegory are, in the first place, together on the temporal side of an opposition between temporal and spatial tropes:

> The temporal void that [irony] reveals is the same void we encountered when we found allegory always implying an unreachable anteriority. Allegory and irony are thus linked in their common discovery of a truly temporal predicament. (1983, 222)

In fact, this formulation is deemed 'dangerously satisfying' by de Man, and only for a moment does he allow temporality to act as the unifying theme for allegory and irony, before irony is returned to its rightful position on the side of spatiality and instantaneity:

> The fundamental structure of allegory reappears here in the tendency of the language toward narrative, the spreading out along the axis of an imaginary time in order to give duration to what is, in fact, simultaneous within the subject.
>
> The structure of irony, however, is the reversed mirror-image of this form. In practically all the quotations from Baudelaire and Schlegel, irony appears as an instantaneous process that takes place rapidly, suddenly, in one single moment: Baudelaire speaks of 'la force de se dédoubler rapidement,' 'la

puissance d'être à la fois soi-même et un autre'; irony is instantaneous like an explosion and the fall is sudden. (1983, 225)

Against the simultaneity of symbol, de Man aligned irony and allegory for the encounter they offered with a truly temporal predicament, but here they are opposite structures, the first of which is associated with narrative duration. The example de Man is using at this point in the argument – some lines from Wordsworth's Lucy Gray poems – fits our purposes well, because it deals with the 'shock of mild surprise' by which the advent of death alters the innocence of what went before: first there was error, then, as the result of a surprise, an insight, a 'stance of wisdom' not possible within the 'actual temporality of experience' (1983, 225) but achievable in retrospect by the poem's speaker. The meaning of allegory is expanding here, in a way that is characteristic of de Man, to the point that it is interchangeable not only with narrative, but also with temporal experience in general, so that the interplay of irony and allegory is nothing less than the dynamic of presence and duration; and here is the point at which the opposition falls back into a fundamental sameness:

> In this respect, irony comes closer to the pattern of factual experience and recaptures some of the factitiousness of human existence as a succession of isolated moments lived by a divided self. Essentially the mode of the present, it knows neither memory nor prefigured duration, whereas allegory exists entirely within an ideal time that is never here and now but always a past or an endless future. Irony is a synchronic structure, while allegory appears as a successive mode capable of engendering duration as the illusion of a continuity that it knows to be illusionary. Yet the two modes, for all their profound distinctions in mood and structure, are the two faces of the same fundamental experience of time. (1983, 226)

We should not yield to the temptation, de Man argues, to value one of these tropes over the other any more than we would value presence over duration, because these are simply the two faces of the same thing, and the 'knowledge derived from both modes is essentially the same' (1983, 226). Against evaluations of the kind advanced by Booth and Kermode, de Man avers that the ironic knowledge apprehended in an instant, of the kind he has found in Schlegel or Baudelaire, could be strung out in time, just as the diachronic wisdom of Hölderlin or Wordsworth could be stated ironically. Perhaps what is most interesting about this general conflation is the way in which it has pushed de Man's argument towards his concluding remarks about the novel, the genre 'which is caught with the truly perverse assignment of using both the narrative duration of the diachronic allegory and the instantaneity of the narrative present' (1983,

226–7). The remarks about this inherent combination are, it must be said, unsatisfying in their brevity. De Man is convinced, for example, that the combination of irony and allegory is simple in cases where 'author and narrator are considered to be one and the same subject' and only a little more complicated when the novel is considered as a structure that 'begins in error but works itself almost unwittingly into the knowledge of this error' (1983, 227). Both of these remarks pertain to the analysis of a straightforward surprise of the kind we are considering without saying much about the interplay of authorial and narratorial knowledge, or the movement from error to knowledge in narrative time. The third and final remark, however, is a little more developed in its account of the combination:

> The real difficulty starts when we allow for the existence of a novelist who has all these preliminary stages behind him, who is a full-fledged ironist as well as an allegorist and has to seal, so to speak, the ironic moments within the allegorical duration. (1983, 227)

His example is Stendhal, an ironist by virtue of his self-contained moments, and an allegorist on account of the way that those moments take their place in novels of duration, where the 'combination of allegory and irony also determines the thematic substance of the novel as a whole, the underlying *mythos* of the allegory' (1983, 228). De Man is speaking here of Stendhal's *Chartreuse de Parme*, a novel that tells the story of two lovers who cannot quite unite because one of them is imprisoned in a tower, and who, through a system of literary antecedents and allegorical episodes, seem to be enacting the condition of narrative itself. In this sense the question of allegory and irony relocates from the mere temporal organisation of novels in general to the thematic particularities of this novel, whose underlying *mythos* is the 'unovercomable distance which must always prevail between the selves', which in turn 'thematizes the ironic distance that Stendhal the writer always believed prevailed between his pseudonymous and nominal identities' (1983, 228).

I have been suggesting that this is an argument that moves too fast, between allegory and duration, irony and presence, tropes and philosophical conceptions of the self; and far too fast through its argument about narrative. The latter first offers the proposition that the combination 'the narrative duration of the diachronic allegory and the instantaneity of the narrative present' is inherent in all novels: 'to try for less than a combination of the two is to betray the inherent *gageure* of the genre' (1983, 226–7). It follows that *Chartreuse de Parme*, by virtue of being a novel, involves some effort of this kind at a combination of the diachronic and the narrative present, of allegory and irony, though at this level of abstraction this seems little more than a claim that present moments and sequences are logically dependent on each other. But de Man's interest lies not only in the temporality of all novels, in the inherent *gageure* of the genre, but also in what singles this novel out: namely, that it happens to be a novel about novels, or that it takes the split in the self, the foundation of irony, as its thematic topic. Here is the ending of de Man's essay in full:

> The novel tells the story of two lovers who, like Eros and Psyche, are never allowed to come into full contact with each other. When they can see each other they are separated by an unbreachable distance; when they can touch, it has to be in a darkness imposed by a totally arbitrary and irrational decision, an act of the gods. The myth is that of the unovercomable distance which must always prevail between the selves, and it thematizes the ironic distance that Stendhal the writer always believed prevailed between his pseudonymous and nominal identities. As such, it affirms Schlegel's definition of irony as a 'permanent parabasis' and singles out this novel as one of the few novels of novels, as the allegory of irony. (1983, 228)

The claim here is that such novels – novels of novels, allegories of irony – are rare, and the further impression is that it is the thematic concern with split selves, allegorised as lovers, yet pertaining at a higher level to the condition of fictional writers more generally, that singles this novel out as an affirmation of permanent parabasis. The structure described here seems, after all, to correspond closely to the account I have been offering of *Fingersmith*, a novel which tells the story of two lovers who, like Eros and Psyche, and Stendhal's Fabrice and Clélia, are never allowed to come into full contact with each other as a result of the unbreachable distance that separates them. In the case of *Fingersmith*, the underlying *mythos* is the same, and although some of the thematic apparatus of imprisonment is at work in the novel (Maud's imprisonment by her uncle; Sue's incarceration in the asylum), the distance between the lovers is primarily based on the inverted perceptions of truth and error that separate them. More than Stendhal's novel, the representation of separated lovers in *Fingersmith* bears directly on questions of the divided self, of the kind that de Man identifies as Stendhal's condition as an author, not only because of their same sex resemblance, but also because the relationship is surrounded by questions of authorship and surrogate authorship, reading and surrogate readers, plotting, stories and books, and its questions of who knows what and when are allegorised in their relationship, as the allegory of irony. If parabasis is conventionally a digression in which an author addresses a reader, the notion of irony as 'permanent parabasis' that de Man finds in Schlegel is not some literary rarity, even less some basis for judgements of literary value, but should be seen instead as the tendency that every romantic thriller displays towards metanarrative commentary, whenever an author hints at the movement from error to knowledge, or shares secrets with a reader. From this point of view, it is interesting to note that the divergence often upheld by critics between basic forms of irony, such as dramatic irony, and its more sophisticated forms, discussed as 'romantic irony', seems to reintroduce an element of valorisation that de Man sought to exclude, for fear that it would obfuscate the structures concerned. It seems irrelevant to argue that the allegorisation of irony in *Fingersmith* in any way guarantees its value, and inaccurate to think of it even as a rarity in numerical terms, since permanent parabasis is an observable feature of any thriller in which time flow is simulated in the combination of movement from past to future and from error to knowledge, and in which dramatic irony is the principal device in the perspectival control of that flow.

Freedom and the Inescapable Future

Many of the perspectives that we have explored on the difference between narrative and life seem to return to what Ricoeur calls the 'paradox of emplotment' which 'inverts the effect of contingency into an effect of necessity'. It has often been said that narrative somehow banishes chance. Leland Monk says this in his study of chance in the British novel, that 'chance is that which cannot be represented in narrative' despite the manifest efforts to do so in the novel of the late Victorian and modern period. Mallarmé, Monk claims, understood that, 'though a throw of the dice will never do away with chance, narrative will' (Monk 1993, 9). But the paradox of emplotment is equally catastrophic for the categories of choice and freedom, as Gary Morson argues, even while the efforts to represent free choice have produced some of the most important developments in modern narrative technique. Yet we are perspectively yoked to people with agency, so that, even if for readers the present is only quasi-present, and the future, by virtue of having been written, is not open, narrative produces a semantic effect of presence in which the activities of desire and intention, action and agency, are shared between readers and narrative participants. We desire, will, plan, resist, hope and fear in a world that is not susceptible to our efforts because we are in the company of participants whose actions, we suppose, have the normal performative effects of bringing the future into being and producing its phenomenal content. The tension between the effort to represent freedom in narrative and the basic condition of its impossibility becomes one of the principal thematic resources of fiction, and this chapter aims to explore this paradox as a thematic as well a linguistic condition.

The question of freedom is announced by Ishiguro's title *Never Let Me Go* as a request for everlasting captivity, and this identifies a basic question to which the novel addresses itself about why we might not only accept but also actually beseech our own confinement. The importance of this question stands out in relief against the triviality of the idiom that expresses it. Ishiguro's novel invents and names itself after a pop song, which belongs to a recognisable category of pop songs, or to a field of imagery, in which the paradox of unwanted freedom is simply the upshot of a conventional comparison of love and confinement: love is a kind of imprisonment that we want, and from which we never want to be freed.

The distance between this serious question and its trivial idiom is traversed in many ways by the novel, perhaps most obviously by the staging of its refrain, 'Baby, Baby, never let me go' as a hermeneutic puzzle. The song's dead metaphor is brought back to life first by Kathy H's literalisation of 'baby':

> What was so special about this song? Well, the thing was, I didn't used to listen properly to the words; I just waited for that bit that went: 'Baby, Baby, never let me go . . . ' And what I'd imagined was a woman who'd been told she couldn't have babies, who'd really, really wanted them all her life. Then there's a sort of miracle and she has a baby, and she holds this baby very close to her and walks around singing: 'Baby, never let me go . . . ' partly because she's so happy, but also because she's so afraid something will happen, that the baby will get ill or be taken away from her. Even at the time, I realised this couldn't be right, that this interpretation didn't fit with the rest of the lyrics. But that wasn't an issue with me. The song was about what I said, and I used to listen to it again and again, on my own, whenever I got the chance. (Ishiguro 2006, 64)

By severing the lyric from its context and making the baby literal, Kathy is able to elaborate a deliberately erroneous, knowingly personal interpretation of an otherwise bland refrain. The hermeneutic puzzle that this presents turns partly on the invisibility of this interpretation to an observer, so that when Madame observes Kathy dancing to the song with a pillow, none of this is apparent. As we discover at the end of the novel, Madame's interpretation of this scene, and of the song's lyric, departs from the blandness of the lyric in a different direction: 'I saw a little girl, her eyes tightly closed, holding to her breast the old, kind world, one that she knew in her heart could not remain, and she was holding it and pleading, never to let her go.' Some of the contradiction, or the paradox of unwanted freedom, is revealed in both of these interpretations, since in each case the captor is imaged as the captive. The first interpretation seems to be an image of a mother held in voluntary captivity, but in danger of being cast off, by her baby. In the second interpretation, a child is in danger of being cast off by the old, kind world which she holds to her breast as if it were her baby. The relations between literal and metaphorical meaning in this hermeneutic puzzle are far from straightforward. In Kathy's own mind, the pillow stands in for a baby, so that the pillow is a metaphor for the baby which is a literalisation of the baby metaphor in the song. In Madame's interpretation of the event there is a kind of double metaphor, whereby the pillow stands for a baby, which in turn stands for a kind old world to which the child clings, so that the baby is a mother and the mother is a baby, and the baby is still a literalisation of the baby metaphor of the song. It is partly the reader's invitation into this prism, with its convergence of, and mutual reflection of, literal and metaphorical meanings, by which the novel develops its most portentous questions about unwanted freedom, where the interpretation of the song acts as an emblem for the novel's central metaphor and its interpretation.

The resemblance between *Never Let Me Go* and the writings of Franz Kafka does not end with the echo of Josef K's name in Kathy H. The literalisation of metaphor, so vividly illustrated in this central hermeneutic puzzle, is a mode of operation which has been used to characterise Kafka: not only a process of turning a concrete situation into a metaphor, but also of metaphors turned into concrete situations, as if the purpose of a narrative were to concretise linguistic idiom such as 'life is a trial', 'faceless officialdom' or 'they're all the same'. The comparison can be pushed further if we think of Kafka's parable of the doorkeeper, that allegory of unwanted freedom which torments Josef K at the end of *The Trial*, or the more general predicament of Kafka's narratives, in which characters accept the unacceptable, treat the grotesque as if it were normal, or confer a kind of homeliness on the most offensive of social injustices. Kafka and Proust are, in fact, the two most prominent references among a small group of writers who are actually named in the narrative of *Never Let Me Go*, and in this pairing we find the conjunction of two species of paradox which organise the novel's themes. On one hand, there is a set of contradictions around questions of freedom and captivity, and on the other, a set of temporal structures in which these issues are embedded. If Kafka's relevance is primarily to the paradox of unwanted freedom, Proust's name can be attached to the family of temporal paradoxes which dominate the narrative voice, such as the recollection of forgetting, or perhaps more prominent still, the recollection of anticipation. It is in this conjunction of unwanted freedom and remembered anticipation that the novel's most sinister observations unfold.

Remembered forgetfulness

Genette's reading of Proust in *Narrative Discourse* is concerned partly with what he calls 'double structures', and which I have been calling tense structures: structures of temporal reference which produce complex versions of the relationship between the time of an utterance and the time to which it refers. There is a sense in which such structures co-operate with certain well-known philosophical accounts of time in human consciousness, such as Husserl's account of the present as a crossed structure of protentions and retentions, or Heidegger's rejection of the present, and preference for anticipation, as the basis for an understanding of human being. The usefulness of a tense structure for narrative, of the kind that Genette gives us, is for the description of structures of temporal reference more complex than any notion of presence can provide, and which are capable of analysing the double structures which characterise all narrative. There is a sense in which tense, or the relation between narrative time and the time of narrated events, is in play in any narrative, and a further sense in which this relation can be deployed for particular purposes by particular novels. In *Never Let Me Go*, time has a particular atmosphere, a kind of doubleness, which shapes all levels of the discourse, from setting to narrative voice. A very general example of this doubleness might be a characteristic that *Never Let Me Go* shares with the Harry Potter novels. The novel is narrated from the late 1990s in England, so that most of its events take place in the last thirty years of the twentieth century, but one of the principal characteristics of the novel is a kind of timelessness, achieved in part by the scarcity of historical locators and specific temporal references. There is the occasional car, and a significant cassette tape, but otherwise the temporal atmosphere pulls away from any identifiable location in the historical present in both directions. There is, on one hand, a sense of the future, which inheres in the novel's interest in cloning; and on the other hand, a sense of the past, in the form of a kind of public school memoir, or a recollection of a childhood apparently isolated from the forces of history.

This odd historical present, with its atmosphere of the past and the future, provides a broad setting for a more precise double structure in the narrative voice, which derives from the relation between narrated time and the time of the narration. Particularly in the early sections of the novel, Kathy, our narrator, is never quite sure of the accuracy of her own narration, as a result of the significant gap between narrated time and the time of narration. The distance of events in time, however, is not the only source of her unreliability; alongside her protestations of temporal distance ('This was all a long time ago so I might have some of it wrong' (p.12)) there are indications of interference in the memory from acts of recollection and narration which mediate between a narrated event and the time of its narration. Just as one often remembers the photograph in place of the event, or the story that one has told of an event rather than the event itself, Kathy consistently indicates that the most distant events in her narration have been remembered before, and possibly told before, to the point of obscuring the events themselves. Her characteristic phrases – 'That was when . . . ' and 'There was the time when . . . ' – suggest a kind of foreknowledge of the events to be narrated, or a community of addressees for whom these events, or the stories of them, are already known. Everything has been told before, and there has often been a collective agreement on a particular version of events.

This constant mediation of events by some act of recall later offers a basic tense structure for the analysis of the narrative voice, a structure of reference that might be called the *proleptic past perfect*. The past perfect is a tense that refers to an event which is previous to another event in the past. In other words, there are three time locations involved: the narrated event, the time of its narration, and a time zone in the middle, and this middle location may be constituted by events which are posterior to the events being narrated, including acts of recollection which are posterior to the events being narrated yet anterior to the time locus of our narrator. This mediating time locus is interesting because it can function both as recollection (in relation to the narrator) and as anticipation (in relation to the narrated), and even as both, as the recollection of anticipation. A simple example of the structure of the proleptic past perfect would be a sentence of this kind: 'Ruth and I often found ourselves remembering these things a few years ago, when I was caring for her down at the centre in Dover' (15). The 'these things' of this sentence refers to events at Hailsham, Kathy and Ruth's school, and which constitute the primary sequence of the narration at this point. But there is also a recollection here of an act of recollection later, between Ruth and Kathy, which takes place a few years before the time of the narration, and this mediating position gives to the past perfect the power also to be proleptic, in this case by referring forward to a time when Ruth is in a recovery centre in Dover, a snippet, or evocation of future time in the narration which arouses the expectations of an as yet unexplained occurrence. A more complex example of this structure can be found in the recollection of a recollection which is not agreed upon:

> We'd been in the middle of what we later came to call the 'tokens controversy'. Tommy and I discussed the tokens controversy a few years ago, and we couldn't agree when it had happened. I said we'd been ten at the time; he thought it was later, but in the end came round to agreeing with me. I'm pretty sure I got it right: we were in Junior 4 – a while after that incident with Madame, but still three years before our talk by the pond. (35)

In this example of the proleptic past perfect, the middle event is again an act of recollection, but there is a disagreement about the time line of the events being recollected. There is also perhaps a more collective 'we', which may refer to a more general community of recollectors who have, since then, named the episode as the 'tokens controversy'. And again, this mediating location in time operates partly as the recollection of recollection, but also as prolepsis, in the excursion it offers into a future event cryptically referred to here as 'our talk by the pond'. It is worth noting also that, in an example such as this, the cryptic flashforward seems to be based in an assumption that the reader shares in the knowledge of future events, or belongs to the community of recollectors concerned, so that prolepsis is an unwitting effect produced in the gap between the assumed and the real reader.

Memory failure is a familiar source of unreliability in the first person narrative voice, and Kathy's constant references to previous difficulties of recollection can be thought of as a subspecies of this kind of unreliability. If unreliability is sometimes marked by protestations of memory failure, this subspecies will also include accounts of prior difficulties and disagreements in remembering:

> This was a long time ago so I might have got some of it wrong; but my memory of it is that my approaching Tommy that afternoon was part of a phase I was going through around that time – something to do with compulsively setting myself challenges – and I'd more or less forgotten all about it when Tommy stopped me a few days later. (12)

The proleptic past perfect is accompanied here by protestations about the difficulty of remembering, but in this example we are presented not only with a recollection of a recollection, but also with a recollection of an act of forgetting. This idea, this apparent paradox, or remembered forgetting, is a recurring feature of Kathy's retrospection. Perhaps the most interesting thing about remembered forgetting is that it requires a subsequent act of remembering in order for forgetting to come into view. In this example, Kathy had more or less forgotten all about the events she is narrating until she was reminded later by Tommy. If memory and forgetting coincide, on the other hand, a more difficult logical problem arises, as St Augustine describes in Book X of *Confessions*:

> I can mention forgetfulness and recognize what the word means, but how can I recognize the thing itself unless I remember it? I am not speaking of the sound of the word but of the thing which it signifies. If I had forgotten the thing itself, I should be utterly unable to recognize what the sound implied. When I remember memory, my memory is present to itself by its own power; but when I remember forgetfulness, two things are present, memory, by which I remember it, and forgetfulness, which is what I remember. Yet what is forgetfulness but absence of memory? When it is present, I cannot remember. Then

how can it be present in such a way that I can remember it? If it is true that what we remember we retain in our memory, and if it is also true that unless we remembered forgetfulness, we could not possibly recognize the meaning of the word when we heard it, then it is true that forgetfulness is retained in the memory. It follows that the very thing which by its presence causes us to forget must be present if we are to remember it. Are we to understand from this that, when we remember it, it is not itself present in the memory, but is only there by means if its image? For if forgetfulness were itself present, would not its effect be to make us forget, not to remember? (1961, 222)

Augustine gets very vexed about this kind of aporia, and it often looks as if there is a simple answer to the problem that so troubles him. It looks here, for example, as if there is a confusion between forgetting as the manner and as the object of a recollection. In one sense there is no problem involved in the act of remembering forgetting but in another there is some reason to doubt that, if I remember what it is like to forget, I am precisely failing to remember the act of forgetting, or remembering as forgetting an experience that was indistinguishable at the time from not forgetting anything. This paradox brings into view a basic characteristic of memory: that it does make present again the experience of a former present, but transforms it into what it was not, in the former present, as a result of the structuring distance of retrospect. This is exactly what the structure of the proleptic past perfect enables, since its triple structure of the time of an utterance, the time to which it refers, and a time between, can accommodate an event, the act of forgetting it, and a subsequent act of remembering that it has been forgotten. It is only when the spacing of these time locations is removed, when memory and forgetting coincide, that they collapse into contradiction.

Recollected anticipation

There is a family resemblance between the idea of a recollection of forgetfulness and the temporal structure which dominates Kathy's narrative, the recollection of anticipation. It is one thing to remember the failure of memory, but something subtly different to remember what the future used to be like, or how one used to envisage it. Kathy's narrative is full of such recollections:

After that morning I became convinced something else – perhaps something awful – lay around the corner to do with Miss Lucy, and I kept my eyes and ears open for it. But the days passed and I heard nothing. What I didn't know at the time was that something pretty significant had happened only a few days after I'd seen her in Room 22 . . . (84)

The family resemblance between remembered forgetting and this kind of remembered anticipation is that the object of the recollection in both cases is an absence of knowledge, and that the recollection of not knowing is impossible except in relation to a subsequent state of knowing. This is most clearly represented in this example by the temporality of 'what I did not know at the time', which contains a movement from ignorance to knowledge. On top of that there is something more complexly proleptic at work here as Kathy remembers becoming convinced that something awful lay around the corner, but the future that she remembers envisaging in this moment of dread is significantly less dreadful than the one which is going to come about, so that the very idea of dread develops an irony produced in the chasm between Kathy's remembered anticipations, and the anticipations made by a reader of the more extreme horrors which lie in wait. Many of the novel's remembered anticipations work in this way, as ironic failures to anticipate the really awful thing around the corner.

To recall what one did not know at the time is to recall in the light of a later event, or an outcome, or to view the past in the mode that is sometimes referred to as teleological retrospect. The mode of teleological retrospect (and I am not convinced there can be any other kind of retrospect) is to explain past events in the light of later events, and therefore to confer on those events a significance that they did not possess at the time of their occurrence. For Kathy, this kind of revision of the significance of events is a feature of many of her sentences:

> As I've said it wasn't until a long time afterwards – long after I'd left the cottages – that I realised just how significant our little encounter in the churchyard had been. I was upset at the time, yes. But I didn't believe it to be anything so different from other tiffs we'd had. It never occurred to me that our lives, until then so closely interwoven, could unravel and separate over a thing like that. (180)

There is anticipation embedded in this recollection, of the unravelling of lives, but whereas in previous examples the prolepsis has been part of a recollection of an anticipation, in this case the memory simply functions in a double structure, as both a memory and an anticipation. The novel, then, constantly projects backwards to remember what Kathy did and did not know about the future, and if it is difficult to remember what one did know, it is much more difficult to remember what one did not:

> So why had we stayed silent that day? I suppose it was because even at that age – we were nine or ten – we knew just enough to make us wary of that whole territory. It's hard now to remember just how much we knew by then.

We certainly knew – though not in any deep sense – that we were different from our guardians, and also from normal people outside; we perhaps even knew that a long way down the line there were donations waiting for us. But we didn't really know what that meant. (63)

Though there are many moments in which Kathy considers openly in this way what she did and did not know of the future in the past, more commonly, questions of what Kathy knew operate as a distancing device between character and reader, as a gap begins to open between her own remembered false anticipations and our own increasingly accurate ones. The narrative also deploys a temporal strategy which brings together our two temporal paradoxes of remembered forgetting and recollected anticipation in which hope is seen to depend upon an act of forgetting:

Maybe once Hailsham was behind us, it was possible, just for that half year or so, before all the talk of becoming carers, before the driving lessons, all those other things, it was possible to forget for whole stretches of time who we really were; to forget what the guardians had told us; to forget Miss Lucy's outburst that rainy afternoon at the pavilion, as well as all those theories we'd developed amongst ourselves over the years. It couldn't last of course, but like I say, just for those few months, we somehow managed to live in this cosy state of suspension in which we could ponder our lives without the usual boundaries. Looking back now, it feels like we spent ages in that steamed up kitchen after breakfast, or huddled around half-dead fires in the small hours, lost in conversation about our plans for the future. (130)

The act of recollection in such delusional moments is a recollection of two absences: the absence of memory in forgetting, and the absence of knowledge of the future in hopeful anticipation.

It is not only at the level of the tense structures of the narrative voice that such false hopes are developed. Memories of false hope, and the false idea of a dream future, also run through the novel at a more obviously thematic level. One example is the theory of 'possibles', a word used by the Hailsham students to refer to those people in the outside world from whom they may have been genetically copied. With an echo of Jean-Paul Sartre's account of the future as the realm of pure possibility and therefore freedom, the idea of the 'possible' for the students is a living vision of the future:

Then there were those questions about why we wanted to track down our models at all. One big idea behind finding your model was that when you did, you'd glimpse your future. Now I don't mean anyone really thought that if your model turned out to be, say, a guy working at a railway station, that's what you'd end up doing too. We all realised it wasn't that simple. Nevertheless, we all of us, to varying degrees, believed that when you saw the person you were copied from, you'd get some insight into who you were deep down, and maybe too, you'd see something of what life held in store. (127)

Something of the technique of literalisation, or concretisation, can be seen at work here, where the notion of possibility is incarnated and available to vision. As both a model and a future, the 'possible' is the reification of an ideal. Ruth, for example, has a dream of working in a glass-fronted office in her ideal future, and when the students go to Norfolk in search of her possible, a strange confusion is created between her genetic source and a more general reification of her hopes. The episode also gives rise to an opportunity for a reified double time structure of the kind that we have been observing in tense structures; as the location of Ruth's possible, Norfolk functions as a protention of the future, but it also functions in the novel as a place of retention – a place, the students believe, in which everything that has been lost in the past will reappear in the future. To this double structure belongs the rediscovery of Kathy's cassette tape, and its injunction for the future – never let me go.

I argued at the end of the last section that the proleptic past perfect allowed for a kind of spacing between remembering and forgetting, and that this spacing produced temporal distance between contradictory elements that, if they were to coincide, would collapse into contradiction. The same argument can be made for the temporality of the remembered false anticipation, or for the self-deceit involved in the hope of an ideal future. If we think about confession generally, the temporal gap between the narrator and the narrated is often a moral gap, a distance in time which allows the narrator a moral distance on what a sinner he used to be. The problem in confessional structures like this is that, as the narrative progresses, the time gap between the narrator and the narrated diminishes, and with it, the moral distance between the narrator and the narrated threatens to disappear. We depend, in confession, on being able to trust the narrator about what an untrustworthy person he used to be, and cannot allow the untrustworthiness to spill over into, or coincide with, the time of narration. It is no surprise that, in texts like Augustine's *Confessions* and Proust's *In Search of Lost Time*, at the moment of coincidence, when the story being told catches up with the time of its telling, the narratives erupt into philosophical discussions of the nature of time. An alternative possibility, perhaps, is to allow the reliable time locus of the narrator to become contaminated with the deceits and delusions of the narrated. The question we must ask in *Never Let Me Go* in this regard is this: at what point do these false anticipations transform into reliable ones? At what point does falsity transform itself into truth?

Though there is clearly a slow process of realisation, of coming to knowledge, in the novel's forward movement, we also regularly see Kathy in the novel's 'now', in the time of narration, still falsely anticipating the future. At the beginning of the novel, she tells us: 'I won't be a carer any more come the end of the year, and though I've got a lot out of it, I have to admit I'll welcome the chance to rest – to stop and think and remember' (34). It certainly looks here as if the false anticipations continue untransformed. For Kathy, to stop being a 'carer' means to start her 'donations', or in a less euphemistic language, to die a premature death. The very persistence of this euphemistic language supports the supposition that the truth of what happens for Kathy at the end of the year is not being honestly apprehended, and that the horror of realisation is averted in cheerful optimism. Likewise, at the end of the novel, by which time the reader has developed a full understanding of this horror, we see Kathy extending the delusion in her anticipatory remarks: 'by the end of the year I won't be driving around like this any more' (262). It is towards the collapsing of the gap, the conflation of narrated time and the time of narration, or the contamination of an honest recollection with the delusions that have been recounted, that the memory of anticipation points.

Privileged deprivation

The paradox of unwanted freedom from which I began and the temporal paradoxes of remembered forgetting and the recollection of anticipation can be brought together by a third paradox which presides over the novel – the paradox of privileged deprivation. This idea, of a sense of privilege around the condition of atrocity in which Kathy and the others find themselves, is one of the most striking features of the novel. It offers an answer to the question: to what end is the temporal structure that I have been analysing deployed in *Never Let Me Go*? But it also serves as an answer to some of the more basic responses to Kathy's passivity, and to the mystery of her unwanted freedom. Why doesn't Kathy run away? Why, after she is freed from Hailsham, does she not save herself?

One way of answering such questions is with reference to a theory of social control which relates particularly well to the total institution – that is, the kind of institution which does not let you go home in the evening, like a prison, or the army, or perhaps most relevantly, a boarding school – known as 'relative deprivation'. In its most abstract form, the theory of relative deprivation can be understood in the following way:

A is relatively deprived of X when (i) he does not have X, (ii) he sees some other person or persons, which may include himself at some previous or expected time, as having X, (whether or not this is or will be in fact the case), (iii) he wants X, and (iv) he sees it as feasible that he should have X. Possession of X may, of course, mean avoidance of or exemption from Y. (Runciman cited in Wakeford 1969, 69)

The key feature of this concept of social control is that a person who enters a total institution must be systematically deprived of individual freedom, personal space, and opportunities for self-expression relative to other individuals in the institution. The privilege of others must therefore be made visible and possibly offered as an enticement to an individual, as an expectation for the future. This initial deprivation must be relieved slowly over time, often as a consequence of seniority itself (that the mere serving of time will ensure some relief from deprivation), but also as a reward for conformity to the institution's rules and values. In this way, relative deprivation creates an entirely internal economy of privilege and deprivation, where comparisons are not relative to the general population or standards in the outside world. As a socialisation process, the function of relative deprivation is observed in effects on behaviour and values which survive the experience of the total institution itself, and which persist in life afterwards. Such effects might include a generalised legitimation of social inequality, or a feeling of privilege in relation to conditions perceived by others as deprived.

The control of time is central for relative deprivation in a number of ways. If we take a boarding school, for example, it is in the rigid control of daily routines that deprivation is most directly controlled, with each day and each week being divided into time zones of varying degrees of constraint: periods or work and play, of being in and out of houses, of being silent and being allowed to speak, with frequent assemblies for roll calls and inspections. Over longer time periods the rigorous constraints of daily time will be slowly relieved, so that initial levels of relative deprivation yield to greater degrees of freedom, of free periods in the day, and of the freedom to move in privileged ways around the school. A written code of rules will normally enforce a wide range of prohibitions, on personal possessions, on geographical movement, on the use of public and personal transport, on social contact with the outside world, on listening to music, on what you can wear and to whom you can talk. School rules will normally encode a highly visible relief from prohibition, or a system of privileges which entail the removal of basic constraints on freedom. In *Never Let Me Go*, Hailsham is exactly this kind of total institution: an elaborate system of prohibitions and privileges, of constraints upon and opportunities for personal expression. At times,

Hailsham exerts an entirely plausible control over daily time, as, for example, in the very limited opportunities it presents to its students for private conversations. Such interactions have to take place in lunch queues, by the pond, in whispered moments and always with great difficulty. At other times, Hailsham represents a subtle exaggeration of boarding school practices, and a kind of comic literalisation of recognisable aspects of the total institution. One of the crucial features of the public boarding school, for example, is that students are separated from their parents, and that parental functions are replaced by institutional figures such as matrons and housemasters. In *Never Let Me Go*, the separation from parents is exaggerated into the literal parentlessness of a community of clones. Similarly, a typical prohibition like a rule against smoking, a rule which removes the freedom to damage one's own body, is given an exaggerated importance at Hailsham because, for a community of clones being grown for their body parts, smoking amounts, in a literal way, to the corruption of somebody else's organs.

The most important effect of relative deprivation as a socialisation process, in which notions of time and notions of control are most closely forged together, lies in the ability of the total institution to control behaviour in the future, after the constraints of the institution have been removed. In *Never Let Me Go*, this post-institutional world is represented by 'the Cottages', a kind of transitional institution clearly imaged as a university:

> If someone mentions the cottages today, I think of easy-going days, drifting in and out or each other's rooms, the languid way the afternoon would fold into evening then into night. I think of my pile of old paperbacks, their pages gone wobbly, like they'd once belonged to the sea. I think about how I read them, lying on my front in the grass on warm afternoons, my hair, which I was growing long then – always falling across my vision. I think about the mornings waking up in my room at the top of the Black Barn to the voices of students outside in the field, arguing about Kafka or Picasso. (109)

In this spoof of college nostalgia, there is momentary freedom from the control of time, in which the future is not thought about, and the past forgotten. And yet, in this realm of apparent freedom, a mysterious post-institutional force limits the way that this freedom is apprehended and used. Kathy continues to be controlled by the routines to which she has become accustomed at Hailsham in this new realm of freedom, and continues to expect a future which we know, by now, is not the one that lies in wait for her. She has been designated as a carer, rather than a donor, in the Cottages, so that she thinks she is privileged when, in fact, she is doomed. This internal difference between carer and donor not only prevents comprehension of her true situation, but seems to act as a continuing prohibition on interaction with others in the world not governed by such distinctions. To this project – the internal system of comparisons of relative deprivation – we might also attribute the closed community of the novel's characters, the absence of outsiders, and the closed circle between the narrator and her addressees; Kathy continually addresses her narrative to other graduates of total institutions on the model 'I don't know how it was where you were . . . '. And this highly introverted focus is also an explanation of the novel's extensive lexicon of euphemisms: a vocabulary known only to inmates, which names as 'guardians', 'training', 'students', 'carers', 'donations', 'deferrals' and 'completion', a brutal reality more properly named as captors, socialisation, clones, prefects, enforced organ donations, false hope and death.

It is for the maintenance of this gap, this chasm between two realities, one a closed institution, the other a brutal domain of inequality and social injustice, that the temporal structures of remembered forgetting and recollected anticipation are deployed. The time structure of the novel functions as a control of distance, keeping the reader yoked to Kathy, close enough to the truth to experience the process of relative deprivation with her, and yet not so close as to prevent judgement of her, or to be able to see the truth of what is coming to her in the future. The proleptic past perfect, with its oscillation between a half-forgotten past and a falsely anticipated future, is therefore a mechanism for the management of the relationship between knowing and not knowing, and more specifically between knowing and not knowing what the future holds. The temporality that it creates – the slow acquisition of a privileged deprivation, the diminishing gap between delusion and truth – acts as an explanation for why we sometimes accept the unacceptable, or why we sometimes not only accept but actually beseech our own confinement too: because relative deprivation causes us to misapprehend social injustice as privilege. Speaking of Proust's anticipatory recalls and retrospective advance notices, Genette remarks that 'When later is earlier, and earlier later, defining the direction of movement becomes a delicate task' (Genette 1980, 83). In *Never Let Me Go*, we can never satisfactorily separate the anticipation of retrospection from the recollection of anticipation, or prolepsis from analepsis, as if something of the asymmetry of time has been removed by the novel. More specifically, the proleptic past perfect casts us into an uncertain middle, or a location in time which is uncertain about what did happen and what will happen, and the complex tense structures which cast us backwards and forwards make the distinction between the anticipation of recollection and the recollection of anticipation difficult to uphold. A final paradox might, then, be offered as a point of convergence for this issue about the temporality of narrative and this theme of accepting social injustice: the paradox of a future which already exists, that is the open future of the novel, of any novel, a future which lies in wait for us to reach it, and from which there is no possibility of freedom.

Chapter 10

The Philosophy of Grammar

This study began from Genette's notion that we should organise the analysis of narrative around categories borrowed from the grammar of the verb. It is now possible to be specific about what must be added to a grammatical approach if we are to do any justice to the complex philosophical approaches to the future that we have been exploring, and to the particular valence of the unexpected. We found, in each section of the argument, a tight complementarity between thinking forwards and thinking backwards, that the cognitive functions of prospect and retrospect are difficult to separate, and that surprise has a special power to reveal this complementarity. We explored the metaphorical basis for a profound confusion between the spatial orientations of forwards and backwards in our thinking about time. We found, in Morson's analysis of narrative and freedom, the view that foreknowledge makes us hold the forward movement of experience and the backward movement of explanation together in a double structure, and in Sternberg's narratological account of surprise, the notion that the unexpected arrival from the future springs an unexplained past. In Paul Ricoeur, we found that unexpected events in narrative present a paradox which inverts the effect of contingency into the effect of necessity, turning chance into fate and the accidental into the intended, as well as a circular account of mimesis that shows how this paradox refigures our understanding of surprise in life. We traced a kind of oscillation, in thinking about the present and the contemporary, between the notion of the unexpected and the backwards and forwards movements of the future perfect, or the future anterior. We found, in Derrida's notion of the messianic, a proposition that the unexpected event contains within it two different conceptions of time, the first based in what it is like to experience the unexpected, and the other in what it means to understand the unexpected in retrospect. In the notion of peripeteia, we followed a tradition of thinking about surprise as the stringing out in time of irony, and a tendency in narrative to transpose the temporality of peripeteia, by retroaction, into co-presence. And we analysed the distribution of information in narrative as a double structure within which the transaction between anticipation and memory is controlled. In each case, we can say that the tension between prospect and retrospect derives from a core paradox in thinking about time, and in each case the unexpected event is what brings the two apparently incompatible approaches to time, the tensed and the untensed, into view. At each stage, the argument has been concerned with the notion of narrative as a mode of cognition, a way of understanding how the mind works, and particularly how it works when it comes to projecting into the future. Thinking ahead, narrative seems to tell us, is indistinguishable from looking back; we think ahead by imagining looking back; we try to impute to the future the certainty of retrospect. The unexpected event, however, reasserts the asymmetry of time and the basic condition of unforeseeability.

Against this background, then, it is possible to be more specific about what it is that the grammar of the verb can and cannot capture. The question has a currency because, to the extent that it is being asked at all about the temporality of narrative in contemporary criticism, it is being asked in ways that derive directly from, but also go much further than, Genette's proposed borrowings. There is in recent postclassical narratology an attempt to develop the borrowings from grammatical tense of the kind that is outlined for us by Genette, and a significant part of this attempt is the incorporation of further dimensions of the grammar of the verb, of the kind discussed in Part 2, such as those of modality and aspect, especially for the analytical resources that they bring to questions of futurity in narrative cognition. An excellent example can be found in Uri Margolin's contribution to one of the manifesto publications of postclassical narratology, David Herman's volume *Narratologies* (1999). Margolin is looking for an underlying framework that would help us to understand the linguistic manifestations of our experience of things in time, and offers Tense-Aspect-Modality (TAM) as the basic model:

> The basic tenets of this approach are as follows: (1) A narrative can be viewed initially as containing a report about actions, events and states of affairs in some domain or universe of discourse. (2) All reporting is undertaken from a specific viewing position, narrative perspective, subjectivity or experiencing mind. (3) The three basic dimensions of every reporting act are the temporal placement of the event relative to the NOW of the viewing act as earlier, contemporary, or later; the event's temporal contour or inner temporal structure: is it seen from the inside or the outside, as a completed unified whole or as being in progress; and the speaker's modal attitude towards his/her

claims about it: affirmation and certainty (=knowledge), negation, mere belief (=uncertainty), wish, hope or command. (Margolin 1999, 145)

These three basic dimensions therefore do more than just locate the time of an utterance in relation to the time to which it refers. They offer a fuller account of the 'cognitive or epistemic dimensions' that are encoded in language not only by tense, but also by aspectual distinctions (perfective / imperfective, completive / incompletive, simple / progressive) and by modal expressions. The question that I want to ask of this framework is to what extent the addition of aspect and modality moves beyond the classical narratological descriptions of narrative, and by extension, whether it is capable of capturing the expanded notion of the grammar of narrative that I have been espousing.

For Margolin, the limitations of classical narratology often lie in its adherence to a standard view of narrative as 'one which revolves around that which has already occurred and been completed in the story world' (1999, 143). This standard view of narration as retrospection has limited narratology in its ability to describe all of the available narrative options:

> The classical model of narrative, centred as it is on retronarration, and not considering aspectuality and modality as being among the defining factors of each and every narrative proposition, is thus a limiting case of the wider, conceptually richer and more powerful TAM-based model. (1999, 164)

We need to be careful, as Margolin is, with the relation between retrospection as a classical model for what narrative is and the exclusion of aspectuality and modality from narratology. It is not that these are grammatical dimensions of the verb that do not apply to the past tense, nor indeed that retrospection is confined to the past tense, but there is nevertheless an obvious tendency to regard aspectuality and modality, because they convey degrees of completion and certainty in relation to events narrated, as analytical resources especially useful for the description of narratives that are not retrospective. This is, in fact, the burden of Margolin's demonstration: to show that less canonical, or less standard narratives, particularly concurrent narration and prospective narration, are instances where the TAM model acquires its power. In this sense, the classical model of narrative as retrospection is responsible for the general exclusion of aspectuality and modality, since they are less relevant. But, in fact, the general absence of modality and aspect in retronarrative is only one option among others, and one which defines the mode, the particular variety of retrospection of a given narrator:

[In the case of narrative retrospection] . . . all relevant facts are already there, so to speak, and so are their interrelations. The time line of the actions is bounded as regards both initial and terminal phases, and certain and complete knowledge about them can be available to the narrator. Notice that the availability of such knowledge to the narrating instance is itself only an option, and literary retrospective narratives do exist where the narrator dwells instead on his or her lack of knowledge, his or her uncertainty as regards the very occurrence or nature of some crucial past events. On the other hand, retrospective narration is the only form of narration where unqualified factive claims can dominate and unequivocally define the story world. This is actually one of, if not *the* one specific defining feature of retronarration, so it is only natural that most authors employing this temporal stance would also employ this mode. (1999, 147)

We can see, then, that Margolin wants to, as it were, loosen the grip that retronarration has upon our analytical model, but also wants to define retrospection in terms of the prevalence or dominance of the 'factive mode'. A possibility, or an option ('certain and complete knowledge *can* be available,' 'factive claims *can* dominate'), becomes a definition: it is one of the features, and then immediately (in the modality of the 'if not') *the* one defining feature of retronarration. One of the things that comes into view here is the limitations of the TAM model, because it locates the question of certainty in the grammar of the verb, to account for some of the most basic effects of retrospection, and temporal perspective more generally. We have seen, with Sternberg, that the unexpected event 'springs an unexplained past', and that the degree of unexpectedness will often depend exactly on the degree of certainty with which events anterior to the unexpected event have been established. The very alignment of factivity with retrospection is one of the things that narrative surprise characteristically overturns, when we discover that everything we thought to be the case about the past was based in a limited or false understanding. What TAM can speak of, beyond the temporal relation between a narrative speech act and the time of events, is the relations of completion and certainty that pertain between a narrator and events, of their grammatical encoding, but cannot capture the movement over time in which uncertainty transforms into certainty, or certainty into uncertainty. What this means is that, in the quotation above, when Margolin reflects upon the exception to the rule that retronarration deals in certainty, he asks us to notice those cases where the option to make complete and terminal knowledge available to the narrator has been refused, and where the narrator 'dwells instead on his or her lack of knowledge, his or her uncertainty as regards the very occurrence or nature of some crucial past events'. These are, of course, the cases where uncertainty actually corresponds to the surface grammatical features of narrative sentences, but they depend upon the concurrence of narration and uncertainty. Yet it is one of the founding suppositions of narrative retrospection that, though complete and certain knowledge is available to the narrator at the time of narration, it is withheld for the purposes of fidelity to the time of narration, to what was and was not known at the time of events by a narrative agent, so that it is exactly the non-concurrence of uncertainty with the narrated events that characterises the stance of retrospect. Any grammatical model that aims to analyse surface grammatical features of narrative sentences will confine itself in this way to intrinsic aspects of narrative voice and so to those aspects of narrative temporality that can be read at the level of the verb.

Margolin is alert to the dangers of borrowing so directly from the grammar of the verb, and reminds us regularly in his discussion that 'there is of course no 1–1 mapping between surface grammatical features and the underlying semantic, cognitive, or pragmatic factors' (1999, 146). The caution is related to a widespread recognition in contemporary linguistics that the correlation between time and tense is inexact, and that we can, for example, refer easily to the past in the 'historical present'. Some of the final questions that I want to pose are related to this recognition, and to the need to extend it. Can we also say, for example, that it is easy to refer to the future in the past perfect, or to the past in the future tense? Is the lack of an exact relation between time and tense also true for aspectuality and modality, in the sense that we can refer to the incomplete in completive grammatical forms, or to the uncertain in a factive mode? If Margolin is right, as I think he is, to insist on the absence of any such one-to-one correspondence for all three factors of the TAM model, what, then, do we mean by tense, aspect and mode at a level higher than that of the form of the verb?

One way of answering this question is with reference to a key tenet of postclassical narratology which effectively brings the surface grammatical features of a discourse into contact with the act of reading. A typical statement of the tenet is this one provided by Teresa Bridgeman in her account of a cognitive approach to prolepsis:

> If we consider the act of reading, then, to involve the construction of mental representations of the world, where the reader builds, updates, and modifies local and global models of the fictional world in a dynamic process, then prolepsis has a particular function, in that it cues a piece of the puzzle which can be situated only provisionally in relation to the current state of the reader's global world model. (Bridgeman 2005, 129)

Most important here is the emphasis on the act of reading as a dynamic interaction between the cues of verbal structure and the constantly updating mental representations involved in their comprehension. To speak in this way about the reader's construction of mental representations of a story world is to add a significant dimension to concepts of tense or, for that matter, to aspect and mode. For Bridgeman, the cognitive study of literature too often fails to consider directly the temporal dimensions of engagement with narrative texts, and she finds in prolepsis a topic which highlights those areas of cognitive investigation 'which relate to text processing and memory, and those which offer a theory of the construction, maintenance, and modification of mental representations of worlds over time' (2005, 128). We might remember here that prolepsis belongs to Genette's tense framework in which he moves beyond the grammar of verbs, or borrows from them in order to lift anchor from the encoding of temporal placement in the verb. Temporal engagement is an activity of comprehension which may or may not take its cue from the grammar of the verb; as an act of text-processing that takes place over time it responds to textual cues but it also situates those cues in relation to the 'current state of the reader's global world model'. Bridgeman draws on the work of Catherine Emmot in *Narrative Comprehension* (1997) mainly for its emphasis on the contextual frames that we open up, close down and recall as we read, and which 'enable us not only to track protagonists around the fictional world but also to identify different knowledge states . . . at different stages in a protagonist's life' (2005, 130). One of these frames, the one that puts the 'cognitive' in cognitive narratology, I would suggest, is exactly the 'reader's global world model', the frame that expands narrative tense beyond the temporal placement of a narrator in relation to events, or projects it into temporal engagement, which is an interaction between the complex time structures of a narrative discourse and the frame of a reader located in the world.

Having chosen to focus on the 'temporal placement of the event or action relative to the narrative speech act' it would seem at first as if Margolin leaves himself limited scope to deal with temporal engagement of this kind. Yet the discussion of retrospective, concurrent and prospective narration that follows is very mindful of the reader, and, in fact, often seems to be primarily concerned with the states of certainty and uncertainty as they operate on the reader. Speaking first of the retrospective narrator, who sees from outside the whole course of events, he describes the effect on the reader as follows:

> The *in situ* uncertainty of the narrative agents about the significance and subsequent implications of the situations in which they find themselves is replaced by certain knowledge of the backward-looking narrator. Such

constant tension and juxtaposition between two epistemic stances provide the reader of retrospective narratives with the best of both worlds. The reader can thus identify with a narrative agent's momentary situation or predicament, be concerned for this character and involved with his or her mindset at any given moment, and at the same time be superior to the character or detached from it, being given by the narrating voice the full information, gained in hindsight, about this very situation and its future outcome ('how it will turn out in the end'). (Margolin 1999, 160)

Here again is the basic doubling of time that Morson described in Oedipus, of foreknowledge and identification, which for the reader means the best of both worlds, of knowing the future but also understanding what it is like not to know. But whereas, for Morson, the doubleness results from the reader's possession of foreknowledge in advance, Margolin understands it as a function of retrospect itself, without regard for the question of access, of the extent to which a reader is permitted to share in the completed overview of the narrator. Even if, on the framed level, 'we watch narrative agents lead their lives as an unfolding sequence of present moments', and that these agents 'exist in a basic mode of uncertainty, and sometimes also of error and ignorance', on the framing level there is a textual voice 'who can have certain, complete and error-free knowledge of any of the narrative agents' (160). The importance of Bridgeman's notion of engagement between textual cues such as tense, aspect and mode and the textual processing of a reader's mental constructions is that, while the narrator *can* have this complete knowledge, they do not necessarily have it, and more importantly, share this complete and final understanding to very different degrees. Nothing brings this into view more obviously than the unexpected event in retronarration, since it constitutes a moment of recognition that we have not been permitted to share in the narrator's complete knowledge and understanding.

This is a simple point, as familiar to us as the distinction between concurrent or dramatic irony on one hand, and linear or retrospective irony on the other, but it helps us to identify reasons to refuse the idea that retronarration in any way affiliates itself to certainty, or symmetrically, the idea that concurrent or prospective narration is more faithful to the experiential uncertainties of life. For Margolin it is exactly this unrealistic doubling – the 'dual optics of on the spot AND hindsight' (1999, 161) – that explains the preference among contemporary writers for concurrent narration over retronarration:

One can think of several reasons why contemporary artists have embraced this much more limiting mode. The first has to do with a view of reality itself, the object of knowing as devoid of any underlying unifying macro patterns or overarching regularities, as consisting of nothing but more or less random sequences of momentary events and states, with at most local connections between them. Another motivating factor could be an epistemological or psychological assumption about the working of the human mind, about what and how much we can know and in what ways. The view then is that we are always in the midst of things, that our process of knowing is not only ongoing but also fragmentary, consisting of a succession of moments with their highly incomplete and often hypothetical information and that this succession of partial glimpses cannot be cognitively integrated into a meaningful whole. We are thus always on our way to (*unterwegs zu*, in Heidegger's terms) knowledge, but never there. (1999, 161)

These are perspectives and assumptions rather than truths about the nature of temporal reality and the human mind but, for Margolin, they help to explain why contemporary writers might have rejected retrospect: because it has built in completion of a kind that never reflects the experience of temporal becoming – the incomplete and fragmentary glimpses that never reach some moment of narration where it becomes an integrated whole. This is also the argument that Morson makes about freedom for both Dostoevsky and Tolstoy, that the refusal of retronarration, the preference for concurrence, which Morson prefers to call *sideshadowing*, is an aesthetic choice made in the service of contingency and the open future. Sideshadowing, Morson argues, 'restores the *possibility of possibility*. Its most fundamental lesson is: to understand a moment is to grasp not only what did happen but also what else might have happened' (1994, 119). Margolin and Morson both explain the notion of concurrence from the perspective of aesthetic choice, of the options available to an artist striving to represent the truth of temporal experience, and both, in very different vocabularies, focus on the temporal placement of the narrator in relation to events and actions. Morson describes Tolstoy's view of retrospection as a fundamental falsity, and as part of a system of related fallacies that derive from 'bipolar thinking'. Like Margolin's 'dual optics', retrospection is an unrealistic doubling, full of foreshadowings and backshadowings, which 'draws a straight line from an event in the past to the present situation' and in so doing reduces the constant ravelment of possibilities to causality (1994, 240). A narrator who stands at the shoulder of a character, knowing nothing in retrospect, foreseeing nothing, restores contingency and the possibility of possibility. This is, for Morson, the very meaning of polyphony, and in his discussion on Dostoevsky it is clear that we are talking as much about the temporal placement of an author as of a narrator:

> Polyphony, then, is above all a *theory of the creative process*. The polyphonic novel requires a distinctive kind of authorial activity – one that is both special and perceived as special by the reader . . . polyphonic creation is truly processual . . . When a work is created polyphonically, the eventness it conveys partakes of the real eventness happening during the creative process, when the characters surprise the author. Dostoevsky wrote so as to capture in the final text the thrill of that exciting process. (1994, 98)

The claim here is that an author who is surprised by his characters, who genuinely does not know what will happen during the creative process, will capture and convey that 'eventness' to a reader. In moving from the question of tense (the temporal placement of the narrator in relation to events) to the question of polyphony (the temporal placement of the author in relation to a character) the proposition has changed. Retronarration is no longer a function of tense, but of an author's knowledge of the future in the creative process, and this means that surprise, in this kind of writing, begins in the author as a kind of absence of intention.

A number of problems arise in this kind of thinking about retronarration that underline the need to develop the notion of temporal engagement. These are issues of what is and what is not susceptible, in literature, to grammatical description. This latest question, of polyphony as a theory of the accidental, the contingent or the unplanned in the creative process, threatens to summon all the problems of intention into the debate. At any rate, this question of authorial foreknowledge in the writing process falls clearly into the category of that which is not susceptible to grammatical description, and there are no cues of verbal structure that could establish the presence or absence of foreknowledge. Similarly, if polyphony were to be understood as a species of surprise, the kind conveyed by a lack of planning in contradistinction to the kind that is carefully plotted and controlled, nothing on the textual surface could help us to establish which was which. If retrospection is an unrealistic doubling full of foreshadowings and backshadowings, as Tolstoy saw it, the retrospection concerned is not that which manifests in tense, but rather that which conditions the very dynamic between written narrative and the process of reading it. Why should we assume, for example, that the past tense connotes a future less open than the present tense, or a creative process more plotted and planned? Even if we go up a level from the tense of the verb, why should we take retronarrative to connote certainty or concurrent and prospective narration to have any kind of claim on the authentic representation of temporal becoming when both unfold in the temporality of textual processing, and both are complete in advance? There is a fallacy at work here which, however often it reminds us that there is no one-to-one correspondence between grammatical surface features and underlying semantic and cognitive factors, seeks a foundation for temporal engagement in grammatical objectivities. If there is no one-to-one connection between tense and temporal reference, and no way of distinguishing between polyphony and planning on the basis of temporal perspective, there is also no rational basis for the view that contemporary novelists might better express the experience of temporal becoming by rejecting retronarration.

The question of the future in narrative fiction is not, then, a question about fictions that are about the future, and nor is it about prospective narration. To think otherwise is to confine the question of futurity to its traditional place as a fictional topic or theme, or to bind it to the grammatical forms of prospect. It is, of course, understandable that Margolin should turn to prospective narration as the place where aspect and mood are relevant, since those are the instances in which modal verbs and phrases can be found on the textual surface. But it is also a problem that this limited notion of grammatical description also limits questions about modality, certainty and futurity, and the question of what is to come, to a small sample of narrative examples. These are questions that are more interesting to address in relation to retronarrative, I would suggest, exactly because the one-to-one correspondence of grammar and meaning breaks down and something temporally more complex comes into view. The point can be made simply with reference to a contemporary novel that finds its thematic and formal project in the dynamics of retrospect, such as Julian Barnes's *The Sense of an Ending*. This is a basic surprise narrative, delivering its revelation in the form of an ending that springs an unexplained past: we have been misled, as in *Fingersmith*, by a narrator who has given us no inkling of what he knows from after the endpoint. This is not to say that the retrospect of the narration is unmarked or effaced, as is so often the case in first person narrations, perhaps by the technique of self-focalisation, where the time of the narration recedes behind the foregrounded time of events. Barnes's narrator Tony is a philosophical fellow, who likes to ruminate openly on the nature of time and memory, and who carries around with him, as an adult, the themes and questions that had been opened up by boyhood history classes. The question of certainty is established in the early sections of the novel: 'History is that certainty produced at the point where the imperfections of memory meet the inadequacies of documentation,' Finn declares, quoting a historian invented for the purposes of formulating the novel's central position on narrative retrospect in general. This question of certainty, without documentation or reliable memory, quickly spills over into the main plot, in which Tony struggles to remember and explain the event of his friend Adrian's suicide. Not all novels with surprise endings will indulge in open theorising on the subject of lived experience and retrospect, or on the themes of documentation and corroboration that preoccupy Tony, but they will all enact the same dynamic between the surprise to come and the reinterpretation that ensues. There are, in other words, passages of open self-commentary that bring into the thematic foreground a set of issues about the temporality of any novel, as well as the act of explaining any surprise. The surprise in question is anagnorisis rather than peripeteia in so far as it turns on the protagonist's recognition of a fact, the ignorance of which has been a foundation for his misunderstanding of everything. The moment of overturning, in this case, is above all a moment that renders the comprehension that readers have built of the narrated world incorrect. I would like to conclude with a consideration of the extent to which this most basic of narrative effects is or is not susceptible to grammatical description, and by extension, whether the question of the modelling of temporal becoming can be related at all to the surface grammatical features of the text.

The surprise ending does not always have the effect that it has in Barnes's novel. We might wish to distinguish here between the surprise that provides an unexpected but nevertheless intelligible closure to the novel's action and that which subverts the intelligibility of the sequence through which we have been progressing. We might think here of Ingarden's account of temporal perspective, which divides the cognition of the literary work between the two perspectives of *during reading* and *after reading*, and argue that, in the case of the second kind of surprise ending, these two perspectives are contradictory; the perspective that we reach at the end of *The Sense of an Ending* invalidates the whole process of building, updating and modifying what Bridgeman called our mental models of the fictional world. We are forced, in cases like these, and as many of the novel's reviewers have observed, to reread the narrative for the purpose of correcting all those mistaken inferences and misguided anticipations that comprised the act of comprehension during reading. Only on rereading do we have what Margolin described as the best of both worlds – the dual optics of on the spot and hindsight. This is the significance of Kermode's argument, in his own *The Sense of an Ending*, that peripeteia is the equivalent in narrative of irony in rhetoric, and of de Man's argument in 'The Rhetoric of Temporality' that the only difference between them is that, in the case of peripeteia, the two perspectives do not coincide. Hence, the cognition of the work of art during reading and the cognition of the work after reading are in a relation of temporal disjunction, and necessarily so, since their coincidence, the simultaneity of the perspective during reading and the recognition that invalidates it, would produce contradiction, but contradiction of a kind no more catastrophic than the ironic structures of narrative that permit us to live alongside a fictional character and, at the same time, know what is to come. It is, in other words, a kind of flight from simultaneity and contradiction that gives narrative its cognitive purchase. It is one of the most palpable aesthetic effects of unexpected moments in fiction that they present the experience during reading and the completed knowledge that comes after reading together, simultaneously, in the moment of realisation. The moment itself, however, is one of annihilation, in which everything that has happened is cancelled, contradicted and displaced. In Barnes's novel, the moment of anagnorisis occurs in a scene of comic banality, amidst a scene in which the protagonist argues with a barman about the difference between thin and fat chips:

> 'Then I think you don't understand.' At least he put it differently from others.
> 'I don't?'
> 'Mary isn't his mother. Mary's his sister. Adrian's mother died about six months ago. He took it very badly. That's why he's been . . . having problems lately.'
> Automatically, I ate a chip. Then another. There wasn't enough salt on them. That's the disadvantage of fat chips. They have too much potatoey inside. With thin chips, not only is there more crispy outside, but the salt is better distributed too. (Barnes 2011, 148)

The unexpected, the contradiction of everything that arrives as complete knowledge, produces nothing at all. At least not yet. Several sentences later, the contradictions come into view and the revisions begin: 'And later, at home, going over it all, after some time, I understood. I got it' (2011, 148). But in the moment, while the negation and the narration coincide, there is nothing but flight from the recognition into the banality of chips and salt. This is what I take the novel to be saying about memory and presence, not that unexpected moments are difficult to grasp, but that, in being difficult to grasp, they reveal the structure of time more generally, as a flight from presence, and so the ungraspability, the nothingness, of presence in general.

We can conclude with three points that speak to the philosophical scope of grammatical description. First, it must be a mistake to associate retronarration with a particular epistemic stance because the question of temporal placement of a narrator cannot capture the perspectival relation between protagonist and reader. The very fact that this relation can change between a first and second reading is enough to conclude that there can be no determinate connection between the structure of temporal experience in reading and the surface features of the narration such as tense, aspect and modality. It is the expansion of these categories beyond their grammatical meanings that gives them their philosophical scope as well as their narratological purchase. Second, retronarration and retrospect are not the salient issues for the question of a narrative's potential to reproduce the uncertainty of lived experience or the modality of temporal becoming. The factivity of retrospect, understood in the dynamic of temporal engagement, does nothing to foreclose the open future, and reciprocally it is a fallacy that the present tense in any way produces an immediacy that cannot be achieved by retrospective narration. I have been arguing, contra Tolstoy and Margolin, that the very combination of retrospect and futurity is the thing that gives narrative its special place in the encoding of temporal becoming: that the reading of a narrative, governed as it is by the structure of future anteriority, is the very model of temporal becoming as Lacan understood it, of 'what I will have been, given what I am in the process of becoming' (2007, 247). Finally, it can be claimed that the apprehension of time itself depends on structures that allow this kind of cognitive projection forwards from the emptiness of presence to some notional state of retrospect or completion. In this respect, the future anterior is the structure, in narrative as in temporal becoming more generally, that makes the unexpected intelligible.

Bibliography

Aristotle (1984) *The Complete Works of Aristotle*, ed. Jonathan Barnes, Princeton: Princeton University Press.

Augustine (1961) *Confessions*, Harmondsworth: Penguin.

Badiou, Alain (2000) *Deleuze: The Clamour of Being*, trans. Louise Burchill, Minneapolis and London: University of Minnesota Press.

Badiou, Alain (2006) *Being and Event*, trans. Oliver Feltham, London: Continuum.

Badiou, Alain (2009) *Theory of the Subject*, trans. Bruno Bosteels, London and New York: Continuum.

Barnes, Julian (2011) *The Sense of an Ending*, London: Jonathan Cape.

Bennington, Geoffrey (1990) 'Towards a Criticism of the Future', in D. Wood (ed.), *Writing the Future*, London and New York: Routledge.

Bergson, Henri (2002) *Key Writings*, London and New York: Continuum.

Bigsby, Christopher (2006) *The Cambridge Companion to Modern American Culture*, Cambridge: Cambridge University Press.

Booth, Wayne (1961) *The Rhetoric of Fiction*, Chicago: University of Chicago Press.

Bremond, Claude (1980) 'The Logic of Narrative Possibilities', trans. Elaine D. Cancalon, *New Literary History*, vol. 11, pp. 387–411.

Bridgeman, Teresa (2005) 'Thinking Ahead: A Cognitive Approach to Prolepsis', *Narrative*, vol. 13, no. 2.

Brooks, Peter (1984) *Reading for the Plot: Design and Intention in Narrative*, Cambridge, MA, and London: Harvard University Press.

Byatt, A. S. (1991) *Possession: A Romance*, London: Vintage.

Caputo, John D. (1997) *Deconstruction in a Nutshell: A Conversation with Jacques Derrida*, New York: Fordham University Press.

Casti, John, L. (1990) *Searching for Certainty: What Scientists Can Know About the Future*, New York: William Morrow.

Champigny, Robert (1977) *What Will Have Happened*, Indiana and Bloomington: Indiana University Press.

Collins, Wilkie (2011) *The Woman in White*, London: Simon & Brown.

Connor, Steven (1999) 'The Impossibility of the Present: or, from the Contemporary to the Contemporal', in R. Luckhurst and P. Marks (eds), *Literature and the Contemporary*, London: Longman, pp. 15–35.

Connor, Steven (2012) *A Philosophy of Sport*, London and New York: Reaktion.

Conrad, Joseph (2000) *Lord Jim*, Harmondsworth: Penguin.

Crystal, David (2002) 'Talking About Time', in K. Ridderbos (ed.), *Time*, Cambridge: Cambridge University Press.

Darwin, Charles (2011) *On the Origin of Species*, London and New York: Empire.

Declerck, Renaat (2006) *The Grammar of the English Tense System: A Comprehensive Analysis*, Berlin and New York: Mouton de Gruyter.

Deleuze, Gilles (1972) *Proust and Signs*, trans. Richard Howard, New York: George Braziller.

Deleuze, Gilles and Guattari, Félix (2009) *Anti-Oedipus: Capitalism and Schizophrenia*, Harmondsworth: Penguin.

De Man, Paul (1983) *Blindness and Insight: Essays in the Rhetoric of Contemporary Criticism*, 2nd edn, London and New York: Routledge.

Derrida, Jacques (1973) *Speech and Phenomena and Other Essays on Husserl's Theory of Signs*, trans. D. Allison, Evanston: Northwestern University Press.

Derrida, Jacques (1976) *Of Grammatology*, trans. Gayatri Spivak, Baltimore and London: Johns Hopkins University Press.

Derrida, Jacques (1981) *Positions*, trans. A. Bass, London: Athlone.

Derrida, Jacques (1982) *Margins of Philosophy*, trans. Alan Bass, Brighton: Harvester.

Derrida, Jacques (1992a) 'The Law of Genre', in D. Attridge (ed.), *Acts of Literature*, London and New York: Routledge.

Derrida, Jacques (1992b) *Given Time: I. Counterfeit Money*, trans. Peggy Kamuf, Chicago and London: University of Chicago Press.

Derrida, Jacques (1995) *The Gift of Death*, trans. David Wills, Chicago and London: Chicago University Press.

Derrida, Jacques (1998) *Archive Fever: A Freudian Impression*, trans. Eric Prenowitz, Chicago: Chicago University Press.

Derrida, Jacques (2002) *Without Alibi*, ed. Peggy Kamuf, Stanford: Stanford University Press.

Derrida, Jacques (2006) *Specters of Marx: The State of Debt, the Work of Mourning and the New International*, trans. Peggy Kamuf, New York and London: Routledge.

Derrida, Jacques (2007) *Psyche: Inventions of the Other*, vol. 1, ed. Peggy Kamuf and Elizabeth Rottenberg, Stanford: Stanford University Press.

Dostoevsky, Fyodor (2003) *The Idiot*, London: Vintage.

Downing, Angela and Locke, Philip (2006) *English Grammar: A University Course*, 2nd edn, London and New York: Routledge.

Dry, Helen (1983) 'The Movement of Narrative Time', *Journal of Literary Semantics*, vol. 12, pp. 19–54.

Eagleton, Terry (1986) *Literary Theory: An Introduction*, Oxford: Blackwell.

Eagleton, Terry (2011) *Why Marx Was Right*, New Haven, CT, and London: Yale University Press.

Emmot, Catherine (1997) *Narrative Comprehension: A Discourse Perspective*, Oxford: Clarendon.

Fleischman, Suzanne (1982) *The Future in Thought and Language: Diachronic Evidence from Romance*, Cambridge: Cambridge University Press.

Fludernik, Monica (1996) *Towards a 'Natural' Narratology*, London and New York: Routledge.

Fludernik, Monica (2009) *An Introduction to Narratology*, London and New York: Routledge.

Fukuyama, Francis (1992) *The End of History and the Last Man*, New York: Avon.

Genette, Gérard (1980) *Narrative Discourse*, trans. Jane Lewin, Oxford: Basil Blackwell.

Grosz, Elizabeth (2004) *The Nick of Time: Politics, Evolution and the Untimely*, Durham, NC, and London: Duke University Press.

Hallward, Peter (2003) *Badiou: A Subject to Truth*, Minneapolis and London: University of Minnesota Press.

Hamburger, Kate (1973) *The Logic of Literature*, trans. Marilyn J. Rose, Bloomington: Indiana University Press.

Harvey, David (1989) *The Condition of Postmodernity*, Oxford: Blackwell.

Heidegger, Martin (1962) *Being and Time*, trans. John Macquarrie and Edward Robinson, Oxford: Basil Blackwell.

Herman, David (2002) *Story Logic: Problems and Possibilities of Narrative*, Lincoln, NB: University of Nebraska Press.

Herman, David (ed.) (2003) *Narrative Theory and the Cognitive Sciences*, Stanford: CSLI.

Herman, David (2009) *Basic Elements of Narrative*, Oxford: Wiley-Blackwell.

Hodge, Joanna (2007) *Derrida On Time* London and New York: Routledge.

Holub, Robert (1984) *Reception Theory: A Critical Introduction*, London: Methuen.

Hornstein, Norbert (1990) *As Time Goes By: Tense and Universal Grammar*, Cambridge, MA: MIT Press.

Husserl, Edmund (1964) *The Phenomenology of Internal Time Consciousness*, trans. James Churchill, Bloomington: Indiana University Press.

Huyssen, Andreas (1995) *Twilight Memories: Marking Time in a Culture of Amnesia*, London and New York: Routledge.

Ingarden, Roman (1973) *The Cognition of the Literary Work of Art*, Evanston: Northwestern University Press.

Iser, Wolfgang (1978) *The Act of Reading: A Theory of Aesthetic Response*, London and Henley: Routledge & Kegan Paul.

Ishiguro, Kazuo (2006) *Never Let Me Go*, London and New York: Vintage.

Jameson, Fredric (2002) *A Singular Modernity: Essay on the Ontology of the Present*, London and New York: Verso.

Jaszczolt, Kasia (2009) *Representing Time: An Essay on Temporality as Modality*, Oxford: Oxford University Press.

Jauss, Hans Robert (1982) *Toward an Aesthetic of Reception*, trans. Timothy Bahti, Minneapolis: University of Minnesota Press.

Kant, Immanuel (2005) *Prolegomena to any Future Metaphysics that will be able to Come Forward as a Science*, trans. Paul Carus, Whitefish, MT: Kessinger.

Kermode, Frank (2000) *The Sense of an Ending*, Oxford: Oxford University Press.

Kristeva, Julia [1978] (1981) 'Women's Time', trans. Alice Jardine, *Signs*, vol. 7, no. 1, pp. 13–35.

Labov, William (1972) *Language in the Inner City*, Philadelphia: University of Pennsylvania Press.

Lacan, Jacques (2007) *Ecrits: The Complete First Edition in English*, London and New York: W. W. Norton.

Lakoff, George and Johnson, Mark [1980] (2003) *Metaphors We Live By*, Chicago: University of Chicago Press.

Levinas, Emmanuel (1991) *Totality and Infinity*, Dordrecht: Kluwer.

Luckhurst, R. and Marks, P. (eds) (1999) *Literature and the Contemporary*, London: Longman.

Lyotard, François [1978] (1984) *What is Postmodernism?*, Minneapolis: University of Minnesota Press.

McTaggart, John (1908) 'The Unreality of Time', *Mind*, vol. 17.

Margolin, Uri (1999) 'Of What Is Past, Is Passing, or to Come: Temporality, Aspectuality, Modality and the Nature of Literary Narrative', in D. Herman (ed.), *Narratologies*, Columbus: Ohio State University Press, pp. 142–66.

Matthews, Sean and Groes, Sebastian (2009) *Kazuo Ishiguro*, London and New York: Continuum.

Merleau-Ponty, Maurice (2002) *Phenomenology of Perception*, trans. Colin Smith, London and New York: Routledge.

Monk, Leland (1993) *Standard Deviations: Chance in the Modern British Novel*, Stanford: Stanford University Press.

Morson, Gary Saul (1994) *Narrative and Freedom: The Shadows of Time*, New Haven, CT, and London: Yale University Press.

Muldoon, Mark S. (2006) *Tricks of Time: Bergson, Merleau-Ponty and Ricoeur in Search of Time, Self and Meaning*, Pittsburgh: Duquesne University Press.

Norris, Christopher (2009) *Badiou's Being and Event*, London and New York: Continuum.

Ochs, Elinor and Capps, Lisa (2001) *Living Narrative: Creating Lives in Everyday Storytelling*, Cambridge, MA, and London: Harvard University Press.

Osbourne, Peter (1999) 'The Politics of Time', in R. Luckhurst and P. Marks (eds), *Literature and the Contemporary*, London: Longman, pp. 36–65.

Pavel, Thomas, G. (1986) *Fictional Worlds*, Cambridge, MA: Harvard University Press.

Popper, Karl (2002) *Conjectures and Refutations*, London and New York: Routledge.

Pratt, Mary-Louise (1977) *Toward a Speech Act Theory of Literary Discourse*, Bloomington: Indiana University Press.

Prince, Gerald (1982) *Narratology*, Berlin, New York and Amsterdam: Monton.

Prior, Arthur N. (2003) *Papers on Time and Tense*, 2nd edn, Oxford: Oxford University Press.

Rabaté, Jean-Michel (1990) 'Rien n'aura eu lieu que le lieu': Mallarmé and Postmodernism', in D. Wood (ed.), *Writing the Future*, London and New York: Routledge.

Radstone, Susannah (2007) *The Sexual Politics of Time: Confession, Nostalgia, Memory*, London and New York: Routledge.

Ramo, Joshua Cooper (2009) *The Age of the Unthinkable*, London: Little, Brown.

Rand, Richard (ed.) (2001) *Futures: Of Jacques Derrida*, Stanford: Stanford University Press.

Randall, Bryony (2007) *Modernism, Daily Time and Everyday Life*, Cambridge: Cambridge University Press.

Reid, Rupert (2007) *Applying Wittgenstein*, London and New York: Continuum.

Ricœur, Paul (1984) *Time and Narrative*, vol. 1, trans. Kathleen McLaughlin and David Pellauer, Chicago: University of Chicago Press.

Ricœur, Paul (1985) *Time and Narrative*, vol. 2, trans. Kathleen Blamey and David Pellauer, Chicago: University of Chicago Press.

Ricœur, Paul (1988) *Time and Narrative*, vol. 3, trans. Kathleen Blamey and David Pellauer, Chicago: University of Chicago Press.

Ricoeur, Paul (1992) *Oneself as Another*, trans. Kathleen Blamey, Chicago and London: University of Chicago Press.

Ronen, Ruth (1994) *Possible Worlds in Literary Theory*, Cambridge: Cambridge University Press.

Rousseau, Jean-Jacques (1990) *Dialogues*, trans. Judith R. Bush, Hanover, NH: Dartmouth.

Ryan, Marie-Laure (1991) *Possible Worlds, Artificial Intelligence and Narrative Theory*, Indiana and Bloomington: Indiana University Press.

Simms, Karl (2003) *Paul Ricœur*, London and New York: Routledge.

Stendhal (2007) *The Charterhouse of Parma*, trans. John Sturrock, Harmondsworth: Penguin.

Sternberg, Meir (1992) 'Telling in Time: Chronology, Teleology, Narrativity', *Poetics Today*, vol. 13, no. 3.

Taleb, Nassim Nicholas (2007) *The Black Swan: The Impact of the Highly Improbable*, London: Penguin.

Todorov, Tzvetan (1975) *The Fantastic: A Structural Approach to a Literary Genre*, Ithaca, NY: Cornell University Press.

Todorov, Tzvetan (2000) 'The Typology of Detective Fiction', in D. Lodge and N. Wood (eds), *Modern Criticism and Theory: A Reader*, 2nd edn, London and New York: Longman.

Toolan, Michael (2001) *Narrative: A Critical Linguistic Introduction*, 2nd edn, London and New York: Routledge.

Wakeford, J. (1969) *The Cloistered Elite: A Sociological Analysis of the English Public Boarding School*, London: Macmillan.

Waters, Sarah (2003) *Fingersmith*, London: Virago.

Wekker, Herman (1976) *The Expression of Future Time in Contemporary British English: An Investigation into the Syntax and Semantics of Five Verbal Constructions Expressing Futurity*, Amsterdam: North-Holland.

Williams, James (2011) *Gilles Deleuze's Philosophy of Time*, Edinburgh: Edinburgh University Press.

Wood, David (1990) *Writing the Future*, London and New York: Routledge.

Wood, David (2001) *The Deconstruction of Time*, 2nd edn, Evanston: Northwestern University Press.

Wood, David (2007) *Time After Time*, Bloomington: Indiana University Press.

Žižek, Slavoj (2000) *The Ticklish Subject: The Absent Centre of Political Ontology*, London and New York: Verso.

Index

184   *Index*